The Designer life

STACEY SPELLER

The Designer life

10 STEPS TO TAKE BACK YOUR LIFE AND LIVE!

Copyright © 2018 by Stacey Speller

All rights reserved. This book or any portion thereof may not be reproduced or used in any manner whatsoever without the express written permission of the publisher except for the use of brief quotations in a book review.

Printed in the United States of America

Second Edition, 2018

ISBN 978-0-9798916-4-9 (Paperback)
ISBN 978-0-9798916-5-6 (Ebook)

Speak2Stacey, LLC
10 GlenLake Parkway, Suite 130
Atlanta, GA. 30328
www.staceyspeller.com

Editing and proofreading by Valerie M. Dotson, Ph.D.
(drvaldotson@gmail.com)
Book Cover, Layout and Typesetting by Vanessa Mendozzi

Contents

Introduction	1
Chapter One - A Change In Me	7
Chapter Two - It's all About You	31
Chapter Three - The Company You Keep	53
Chapter Four - Back Down Memory Lane	75
Chapter Five - The Choice is Yours	99
Chapter Six - Play The Hand You've Been Dealt	121
Chapter Seven - What's That In Your Hand?	143
Chapter Eight - Afraid Of The Dark	165
Chapter Nine - Believe You Can Achieve	185
Chapter Ten - One Day At A Time	213

To Dad,
my definition of strength,
courage, and wisdom.

Introduction

Do you want to stop letting life just happen to you and start living life for you? Do you want to stop living life by default? Do you want to stop taking things as they come, and instead have some say as to who and what comes into your life? Do you want to take ownership of your destiny? If you answered *yes*, or even *maybe*, to any one of these questions, then *The Designer Life* is for you.

First and foremost, *The Designer Life* requires your willingness to become an active participant in your life. Now, on the surface, that may seem like a no brainer. After all, if you are not an active participant in your life, then who is? But upon closer examination, you will notice it's not as simple as it sounds. Ponder for a moment who you are, where you are, and how you got there. Think about your goals, your purpose, and how authentic your life really is. You may notice that, perhaps, by passive agreement or simply being an innocent bystander, your life has followed a path not necessarily of your own choosing.

I can tell you, based on my own personal experience, that there was literally a day when I woke up and wondered, "Who hijacked my life?" It was as if I were just going through the motions. I was living each day by putting one foot in front of the other, whether it was managing my carpool schedule, taking a casserole to the sick and shut-in, having a business lunch, meeting with the PTA, or attending a black tie event. I was doing exactly what I thought was expected and / or required of me. And by all accounts, if you took a helicopter view of my life, everything looked great.

Honestly, what more could anyone want? After all, I was living the American dream – the type of lifestyle that has become a world-wide phenomenon on reality television, minus the drama, of course. I had a loving and supportive husband, a son who was a successful scholar-athlete, a house on the golf course, with the best zip code in the state, the right social club memberships, even a well-coiffed, adorable little dog to complete the picture. My life could have easily qualified for the successful, suburban, American of the year award.

Yet, on that fateful morning that I decided to take inventory of my life, I became painfully aware that I had been seized by circumstance. Yes, I felt truly grateful and recognized my many blessings, but I also couldn't help but notice that my life wasn't really going according to plan. Then I realized that I didn't even have a plan. Wow, what a pivotal moment of self-discovery! And then suddenly, without warning, I realized something even more profound. I realized that life doesn't go according to plan if you don't even have one.

Oprah Winfrey has a column in her magazine entitled "This much I know for sure." The premise of the column is to share experiences and describe principles that Ms. Winfrey believes in without a shadow of doubt. Sometimes, in her column, she will interview influential people of interest and put what they know for sure in the column. Well, I can honestly say, "This much I know for sure: life won't go according to plan if you don't have one."

Out of this revelation comes *The Designer Life*. By nature, education and experience, I have very strong research and analytical skills, deductive and intuitive reasoning skills, and a relentless pursuit of truth and knowledge. So I spent countless days, weeks and months doing the research and analysis to determine the best methodology for learning how to design the results I desired for my life because, you see, I had already answered *yes* to all the questions listed above.

Once I began successfully living *The Designer Life*, I began presenting it to audiences and clients. The challenge, however, was trying to convey, in a short period of time, a process that took me several years and is still, in fact, ongoing. Often times I would present *The Designer Life* program, and inevitably people in the audience would want to believe that it is a quick fix, something that could be actualized into a short sound bite equivalent to the amount of time it would take me to describe it during a seminar. I found myself having to emphasize that *The Designer Life* is not something that happens overnight; furthermore, when you really think about it, most things that are meaningful, impactful, and valuable take time and effort.

Then I began to notice that, regardless of the continent, the country, or even the specific demographics of the audience, people wanted to know more. They would either flock to me after I finished, to discreetly ask their questions, or they would send emails wanting to find out more details of my experience and to share their tragedies and triumphs. There were common themes to their inquiries and commentaries that crossed social, geographical, cultural and economic boundaries. I realized that most people really are more alike than different.

So the true catalysts for this book are people just like you, people with a burning desire to be their best and live their best. It is for people who value self-awareness and personal development and who believe that their better days are on the horizon when they chart their own course. So I invite you to begin exploring some new concepts, and some very familiar concepts, presented in a very transparent, relevant, and practical manner. It is my true desire to see you living *The Designer Life*.

CHAPTER ONE

The foundation of *The Designer Life* begins with your consent to make a change, and you only get two choices. Life can either be accepted or changed. If you don't want to change things, then you must accept them as they are. If you don't want to accept things as they are, then you must change them. So if you choose to accept and not change, then there is absolutely no benefit to be derived from reading this or any other personal development book.

Actually, if you are unwilling to make any changes, this would be the time for you to stop reading. Just close the book, and go put it on display somewhere in your house where it will be noticed. Be sure that the book is dusted regularly, and you may even want to fold down a few random pages. Then, when you have guests, you can simply play masquerades for them and pretend that you are invested and interested in growth and self-improvement.

But if you are truly serious and committed to do what must be done, then let's begin with several basic premises. Designing your life will only happen when you can adamantly declare that today is going to be the very last day you wished things were better and simply hoped for a different outcome. A wish is a dream wide awake, and hope is a virtue, not a strategy. Thus, there is no more sitting on the sidelines of your life. Decide that you are not going to wait, wish and hope for the fairytale ending, but you are going to create the outcomes you desire. Everything from this moment forward is about change being a verb, an action that must be initiated by you and for you.

For some it may be a change in attitude, for others it may be a change in their mindset; still others may have to make changes in relationships or habits. And then there are some of you who will need to make changes in every area of your life. It doesn't really matter how much or how little you need to change; the process is the same for everyone, and the starting point is right here and right now.

IF WE DON'T CHANGE THE DIRECTION WE'RE GOING, WE'LL END UP WHERE WE'RE HEADED.

- CHINESE PROVERB -

In order to wrap my arms around this elephant called change, I had to put it into categories, and while the concept of change is vast, there are only four types of change. The first type of change is the change that happens to us. An example of this would be the loss of your job, your home, or your spouse. Basically, it's the type of change you didn't ask for, but it happens anyway.

The second type of change is the change that happens around us. This is evidenced by things like a bad economy, crime in the community, or a country that goes to war. It is also the type of change we didn't seek out or ask for, but it is a product of the world we live in.

The third type of change is the change that happens in us. This type of change is simply a part of the cycle of life that occurs as we grow and mature. This type of change is best understood as it relates to the differences between men and women. On a couple's wedding day, the woman thinks everything will be okay because she will just change him, and the man thinks everything will be okay as long as she doesn't change.

The fourth type of change is the change we initiate because either we don't like where we are, or we realize things could be better, and we want to opt for a more preferred future.

The interesting thing about the four types of change is that there is only one area that is within our control, and that is the change we initiate. Being able to understand the different categories of change will help you discern what you should focus on as you begin designing your life.

> **GOD GRANT ME THE SERENITY TO ACCEPT THE THINGS I CANNOT CHANGE; COURAGE TO CHANGE THE THINGS I CAN; AND WISDOM TO KNOW THE DIFFERENCE.**
>
> - REINHOLD NIEBUHR -

During my personal process for designing my life, I quickly realized that I needed to make some changes. But what took me months to discover was that the change I needed most was not anything I could physically do. Eventually, I began to understand that the first aspect of change was a mental exercise. If I wanted to change my life, I had to change my mind. This was tough for me because I had never considered the power of taking control of my mind; I had always focused on physical disciplines.

My determination had always centered on whatever I physically needed to do. In school, I played tennis, lacrosse, and field-hockey, and I even played on an amateur, adult soccer team. Competition courses through my veins and fuels me to all sorts of physical pursuits. Cycling, running, swimming – I do it all and love it. Just like the motto of The United States Postal Service, rain, sleet and snow have never deterred me from a physical activity. Even my academic success was far more a result of activity, be it researching, studying or whatever was required. Physically, I am a warrior, but mentally, I was a weakling.

I actually never even realized how much I let my thoughts run rampant across the canvas of my mind. In the 1990's, there was a comedian named Robin Harris. His comedy routine focused on urban humor, and an imaginary family he created became an American cultural icon. The family had very ill-behaved children that he called BeBe's kids. They were like little hellions that nobody wanted to see coming. The problem is they would just show up and act unruly because their mother did not provide any structure or discipline to keep them in check. Well, my thoughts were like BeBe's kids, just showing up and acting unruly, wreaking havoc and breaking things because there was no structure or discipline.

About ten years ago, I went to the doctor for a routine physical. Several days after the physical, a nurse called to inform me that the results of my blood test indicated that my white blood cell count was abnormal. The doctor was mildly concerned and wanted to run the test again. The following week, I went in for another blood test. Well, wouldn't you know it; the test results came back on a Friday afternoon. This time the doctor called me and informed me that she was concerned because my white blood count was reading abnormal; therefore, she was scheduling me an appointment with a blood specialist on Monday morning for further testing.

The doctor assured me it was probably nothing, but she wanted to be sure. She just thought it was best to have some additional testing done and have my blood examined by a specialist. Of course, I didn't let anything she said, beyond blood specialist, register in my mind. Something must be gravely wrong. Unfortunately, for purposes of self-diagnosis, the internet is probably one of the worst things ever invented. I immediately began to research every dreadful disease that could possibly be wrong with me based on my white blood cell count.

By Friday night, with the help of the World Wide Web, my prognosis did not look good. I had researched several types of cancers and various blood disorders and came to the conclusion that surely I must have at least one, probably several. I never took into consideration that, other than my doctor wanting me to follow up with a specialist, I had no other data to support my hypothesis.

It didn't matter that I had none of the symptoms of any of those diseases; my mind was off to the races with every conceivable thought of what could be wrong with me.

Now it was time for me to send out my invitations. After all, who wants to contract several deadly diseases all at once and then not throw a huge pity party? So the first person on the invite list was my husband. I told him what the doctor had said and just waited for him to join me in my misery. "It probably isn't anything, Stacey. And besides, you shouldn't spend the weekend worrying. Just wait until Monday, and I am sure everything will be fine." I couldn't believe that my husband could say something so ridiculous. Didn't he know that my negative thoughts were already so far gone that I was preparing my eulogy?

Next on the invite list was my dear friend Vanessa. We had been through a lot together; I knew she would come to my party. After I had explained everything to Vanessa, her response was prayer. Are you kidding me? At this point on Friday night I had at least ten diseases, and she thought she was going to pray for every one of them. I needed someone who would let his or her thoughts run wild like mine. I was going into the depths of despair, and it seemed that the people closest to me were not willing to go with me. How could this be happening?

By Monday morning, I had suffered and died from about twenty different diseases and had been buried and gone on to heaven, all within my run-away mind. When I arrived for my appointment with the specialist, it was merely a formality. As far as I was concerned, I could already hear the angels in heaven playing their harps. After about two hours of testing, I was ushered into the doctor's office, but far be it from me to wait for him to tell me what I already knew. I told him it was okay for him to just tell me the diagnosis straight away. I had done my research over the weekend, and I knew it didn't look good.

The doctor responded with, "Okay then, do you want the good news or the bad news first?" Of course, I wanted the bad news first -- may as well just get on with it, no need to keep the funeral procession waiting. The doctor told me the bad news was the fact that I wasted a perfectly good weekend worrying about nothing. The good news was that I was perfectly healthy. The abnormal white blood cell count was triggered by my bad allergies. I simply sat there partially numb, trying to give my mind time to catch up with what the doctor was saying. There wasn't anything wrong. I didn't have a dreadful disease. Allergies were the problem.

Amazing. My thoughts had just played a very cruel trick on me that wasn't funny. There's a Norwegian proverb that says, "Experience is the best teacher, but the tuition is high." Well, I had just paid a pretty steep price for the lesson I had learned. But later, when I reflected on the whole incident, I developed greater appreciation for both my husband and my friend Vanessa. You see, they already knew the benefit of not letting our thoughts go spiraling into the negative and that prayer is always a positive response to a potential problem.

THE FIRST AND BEST VICTORY IS TO CONQUER SELF.

- PLATO -

The more I tuned into my life and learned about me, the more I recognized that dealing with my mind was going to be the real battle. The same physical energy I was always prepared to exert needed to be channeled into my thought process. The decision for change required me to deal with the space between my ears. I needed a boot camp training program for my mindset because the real power for designing my life wasn't going to come from physical prowess but mental mastery. Change would come from my ability to release potential into my thoughts in order to unleash all the possibilities for my life.

PROGRESS IS IMPOSSIBLE WITHOUT CHANGE, AND THOSE WHO CANNOT CHANGE THEIR MINDS CANNOT CHANGE ANYTHING.

- GEORGE BERNARD SHAW -

The challenge of dealing with my mind was a long process that took quite a bit of time for me to recognize. But for me, once I get something, I immediately move into action. My family and friends jokingly refer to my style as the amputation method. I don't wait to do whatever needs to be done, regardless of what it is. Good or bad, I am going to snatch the bandage off immediately. Yes, it may hurt for a little while, but eventually it will be okay. And, for me, that's better than taking the bandage off slowly and delaying what I deem to be the inevitable outcome anyway.

The amputation method is not for everyone, so as you are reading this, please don't think you have to snatch your bandages off. Everybody is different, and some people prefer a slower process to arrive at their achieved outcome. Several years ago, I had a good friend, whom I'll call Ann, who caught her boyfriend cheating on her. She confessed to me that she knew it was a dead-end relationship. Well, one minute she was giving her confession and the next minute I was counting her among my single friends.

But Ann told me to slow down because she was taking time to end it slowly and that it was easier for her to just gradually wean herself away from the relationship. Months later, the relationship did end. Ann told me she knew it would end but that she just wasn't able to deploy the amputation method like me. She had to go through her process slowly. Even though Ann knew the relationship would end, she wanted to do it bit by bit, taking baby steps until she got to her destination.

Whichever method works for you is fine. There really isn't any right or wrong way; there are just different ways of doing things. I find that it's best not to spend time trying to swim upstream against your natural personality. Rather, focus on how to best improve upon what already exists instead of recreating the entire wheel. Just the idea of becoming aware of how you manage people and situations will go a long way in preparing to design your life.

So with my natural inclination toward the amputation method, I began practicing how to control my thoughts and train my brain. My love of analysis and research really helped me move into my new way of being. I read and examined a myriad of books: the Bible, several works by Mahatma Gandhi and Buddha, writings by the great philosophers like Plato and Socrates, poetry by Shakespeare and Maya Angelou, and even Russell Simmons' book on how he created his hip-hop empire.

IF EVERYBODY IS THINKING THE SAME THING, THEN NOBODY IS THINKING.
- GENERAL GEORGE PATTON -

Changing my mind was important, far too important for a narrow approach. There was no way I could only consider the views of people who thought as I did and were culturally socialized as I had been. I wanted to cast a wide net and understand the thought patterns of a lot of different people. I have always believed that one of the greatest by-products of education is not necessarily agreement, but understanding. Education provides the platform where you can learn about someone or something, even if you totally disagree with the ideology. I believe that to acquire knowledge is far more beneficial than to remain ignorant due to fear of dissent.

KNOWLEDGE ITSELF IS POWER.

- FRANCIS BACON -

The more I learned about the importance of my mindset, the more I began to analyze everyday occurrences. For example, consider how a baby is born. A normal delivery is one in which the baby's head is in position to come out first, not an arm first, or a leg first, but the head first. Modern medicine supports the importance of a baby being delivered head first. When an expectant mother is in labor, if the head is not in position to come out first, there is a very painful procedure done on the mother to turn the baby around. If that procedure does not turn the baby to the head first position, the doctors will deliver the baby by Caesarean Section.

This is all done to ensure that the head is the first thing to break through into the world. In childbirth, once the head is out, everything else follows. For anyone reading this who is skeptical of this concept, simply ask someone who has given birth. I guarantee she will tell you that getting the head out is the most challenging part of the delivery. Once the head comes out, it's much easier to deal with the rest of the body. And that is how I approached *The Designer Life*. I needed to break through in my mind. Once I could get my head birthed into the life I was creating, my body would follow.

When I first began to focus on my thoughts, it was a very conscious and deliberate action. The American Psychology Association has published the importance of thoughts in its medical journals. It is actually a proven scientific fact that when a thought enters your mind, you have thirty seconds before that thought becomes a feeling. So if you have a negative thought that enters your mind, if you don't actively do something with the thought, it becomes a feeling.

So now you are experiencing negative feelings, which do nothing more than generate more negative thoughts. And it becomes a vicious cycle. With negative thoughts becoming negative feelings, you then have to battle both your thoughts and your feelings. Using this model, you could literally think your way into a depression. Conversely, if you have a positive thought, in thirty seconds it becomes a positive feeling, and the same cycle occurs of more positive thoughts and more positive feelings.

But why should I take the American Psychology Association at its word? I started my own personal experiment with this new information. If a negative thought entered into my mind, I immediately countered it with something positive. In the beginning I had to really work at this. I would literally visualize in my mind the removal of the negative thought and the replacement with something positive. I put into practice the theory of "taking every thought captive." And it worked!

The more I learned about how much my thoughts can dictate my life, the more I wanted to learn. There was a certain determination on my part to understand as much as I could and then implement the best possible strategy for living life on purpose and by design. My next area of discovery was that one part of our mind that plays back our history and everything from the past. The other part of our mind pre-plays our future. This was yet another revelation for me. So not only do I make the choice to have negative or positive thoughts, but I also choose if I want to focus on my past or pre-play my future.

Scientifically, nobody can determine which part of our minds we use. Negative or positive, past or future, the choice of how we think belongs to each and every one of us. This was good news to me. It reminded me of when I was a child going for rides in the car with my parents. Invariably, they would pull out their extensive tape collection and listen to what I considered old folks' music. I now realize that what they were listening to was a classical blend of jazz. In any event, I wanted to listen to real talent, something much more enjoyable: the musical greats, The Jackson Five.

Ever the hopeful and persistent one, I would bring my tape collection along, just in case one or both of my parents came to their senses. Most of the time they did not and instead reminded me that the driver gets to play whatever tape he or she wants to listen to. One day they said, "When you are old enough to be the driver, you can play whatever you want, but when you are the passenger, you don't get to control what tape is played."

Well, unlike the tape deck in our family car, you don't have to wait for anything to happen before you decide what is going to play in your mind. The choice is yours right now, today. You can have positive thoughts pre-playing your future. I was excited that this was something completely within my control, and now that I knew it was for me to determine, I resolved to focus on the future in a positive way. After all, there was no point in playing the past; I couldn't go back and change anything; in fact, the only thing I needed from the past was a quick review.

NOBODY CAN GO BACK AND START A NEW BEGINNING, BUT ANYONE CAN START TODAY AND MAKE A NEW ENDING.

- MARIA ROBINSON -

I was willing to spend just enough time playing back the past to understand the lesson in any mistake that had been made. But I certainly didn't want the past to dominate what was playing in my mind. Now that I was equipped with the knowledge of choosing to pre-play my future, that is what I wanted to play. I equated the past to the old folks' music my parents listened to in the car. Yes, they were classics, a part of history, but I wanted to listen to the contemporaries, a part of the future, and I knew exactly what would guide me. "I know what I'm doing. I have it all planned out – plans to take care of you, not abandon you, plans to give you the future you hope for." (The Book of Jeremiah – *The Message*.)

When I learned the importance and value of my thoughts and how much my mindset can influence every other area of my life, I knew I was well on my way to being able to create and shape my destiny. What I want for you is the ability to understand that our minds can be our greatest asset and tool for success when used properly. But the mind can also be our greatest hindrance to accomplishment if we don't manage and control our thoughts. We can waste time and energy focused on the past and the negative. By doing so we can become our own worst enemy, robbing ourselves of a positive future simply by how we think and what we think about. Incorrect thought patterns can place you in a maximum security prison to serve a life sentence with no possibility of parole. Some people become so boxed in that they serve their sentence on death row, believing that whatever life brings them is their lot, and they must simply accept it, like the bumper sticker that says, "Life Is A Bitch And Then You Die."

I don't believe in that bumper sticker, and I don't believe you just accept whatever happens in life until one day it's just over. *The Designer Life* seeks to liberate you from the chains that bind your mind and allows you to see yourself and your life in a positive way. It also helps you to know that in life you may not necessarily get what you deserve, but you will definitely get what you expect.

> **DON'T BECOME A VICTIM OF YOURSELF. FORGET ABOUT THE THIEF WAITING IN THE ALLEY, WHAT ABOUT THE THIEF IN YOUR MIND?**
>
> - JIM ROHN -

Reflections

Change is absolutely essential in creating the life you desire. The most important aspect of change is the changing of your mind because the war will either be won or lost in the battlefield of your mind. You are the only one with the power and authority to deal with your thoughts.

"Summing it all up friends, I'd say you'll do best by filling your minds and meditating on things true, noble, reputable, authentic, compelling, gracious – the best, not the worst; the beautiful, not the ugly; things to praise, not things to curse." (The Book of Philippians – *The Message*.)

Lifestyle Lessons

1. Change is a verb, and it doesn't really matter how much or how little you need to change; it must begin with your consent, and the starting point is right where you are.
2. If you want to change your life, you must begin by changing your mind and recognizing the things that are within your sphere of influence to change.
3. The power to design your life requires mastery of your

thoughts in order to unleash all the possibilities for your purpose.

Design This

Designing your life liberates you from the self-imposed limitations that have kept you bound and allows you to embrace a purpose that is even greater than yourself.

Nothing changes until you do.

Transformation is an inside job; anything else is just a make-over.

Don't try to redefine what needs to be transformed.

CHAPTER TWO

> WE ARE THE ONES WE'VE BEEN WAITING FOR. WE ARE THE CHANGE THAT WE SEEK.
>
> - PRESIDENT BARACK OBAMA -

Years of experience with *The Designer Life* have taught me that when people decide that they are ready to make a change, it's difficult for them to begin working on themselves first. It's actually easier to look at everything and everyone around you as the things that need to change. Most often, we would rather focus on the speck of sawdust in our brother's eye than deal with the plank in our own eye. I must implore you to take the plank out of your own eye, and then you will see clearly to remove the speck from your brother's eye.

Sharon was one of my coaching clients with whom I worked through her employer. She was a mid-level manager in a large accounting firm. Several of the partners believed that Sharon had the potential to one day be an executive within the firm. They wanted to give her an opportunity to further develop some of her strengths and be willing to improve upon some areas of weakness. During our very first session, I asked Sharon to begin considering some areas within her scope of work that she thought needed change and / or improvement.

This was a very general question to get Sharon thinking broadly as we began her coaching. For our second session, Sharon had given thought to the question and had prepared a list of areas in her work that she believed needed to be changed or improved upon. Of the twelve things on her list, ten referred to co-workers and company policy. Sharon was focused externally on what would make her more effective and ready for promotion. She was looking for the company to make personnel changes and change their operations in order for her to be a better employee.

WHEN YOU START DOING FROM WITHIN, YOU'LL FINALLY STOP DOING WITHOUT.

- ANONYMOUS -

The Sharons of the world are not that uncommon. It's human nature to look for change everywhere but within ourselves. We do it in the workplace, with our friends and family, even with our spouses. A classic example of this is found in one of my favorite childhood stories, "The Fable of the Shoe." Once upon a time, there was a king who ruled a prosperous empire. One day he went for a trip to some distant areas of his kingdom. When he got back to his palace, he complained that his feet were in a lot of pain. It was the first time he had gone on such a long trip, and the path was very rough and stony.

The king was very upset that his feet were so sore and blistered and decided he must take action, so he gathered all his subjects together and proclaimed that everyone in the kingdom must work to make sure his feet would not be damaged when he travelled throughout his vast land; therefore, he expected them to cover the entire kingdom with leather. Yes, of course the king knew this would require thousands upon thousands of cows' skin, and the cost to the kingdom would be enormous, but no price was too great for the king.

Then one of his wise subjects dared to make a suggestion to the king: "Why spend so much of the kingdom's resources and have everyone work so hard for years? Perhaps we could cut a small piece of leather and cover your feet?" The king agreed, and that is how shoes were created.

Even though this is a story merely for the entertainment of children, there are actually excellent points that are illustrated. The first point to consider is that when it is time to make changes, start with yourself first. It's easy to point your finger at someone else, but when you do that, the other four fingers are pointing back at you.

Sometimes we can become so over-zealous and want to take on changing the world; we see so much that should be done differently with everyone and everything in our midst. Ambition is good, and there are those who are called to change their community, even their country. And yes, some will change and impact the world, but before you can be that agent of change for others, you must be willing to make changes for yourself first.

SIMPLY REMOVE THE ROCK FROM YOUR SHOE RATHER THAN LEARN TO LIMP COMFORTABLY.

- STEPHEN PAUL -

The second point that the story makes is to always look for the simpler solution first. Sometimes we complicate things to such a degree that we miss the most obvious course of action. Recognize that sometimes you really don't see the forest for the trees, and be willing to step back and look at the issue from a different angle, for when you are willing to evaluate your circumstance with a different view point, you can see the path of least resistance right in front of you.

Change is in the air; you are recognizing that it begins with your thoughts, and now you must begin to sort out those things that need to change. This requires you to take stock of your state of affairs, a thorough and accurate accounting of your life. The assessment must be done with complete clarity and, more importantly, honesty. Take off your rose-colored glasses, get out your magnifying glass, and take a look at your life. Begin to see everything about you as it really is – the good, the bad, and the ugly. You might find that the real you is not necessarily the same you who has been showing up in your life. I call that other you who shows up the representative.

The representative is the person you want everyone to think that you are. He or she can show up anywhere you desire: at the office, at social events, on a date, sometimes even in your marriage. Your representative may have been born in your childhood in an effort to please parents, teachers, and others. Gradually, very subtly over time, you gave birth to your representative without even realizing it. Or your representative may be the by-product of a very conscientious choice to send someone else into your life. Somewhere along the way you recognized some benefit to deploying a different you. Regardless of how the representative came into existence, there is no room for him or her at the table when you begin designing the life you desire. Now is the time that the authentic you must show up.

And the real you requires honesty. It sounds basic enough, but I have done countless case studies with my clients on the lack of honesty in modern culture. People have become so concerned with being politically correct that we have grown numb to giving or receiving truth. After all, we don't want to offend anyone, and we don't want to hurt anyone's feelings, not even our own. The lack of truth and honesty has become the accepted method of operation for most of us.

AND THE TRUTH SHALL SET YOU FREE.
- THE BOOK OF JOHN -

Consider a wife who is preparing to attend a gala with her spouse. Her husband is a bit frustrated with the amount of time it is taking her to get ready and is concerned they may be late. The wife is a bit frustrated with coming to a decision about what she should wear. So, wifey tries on dress number ninety-nine and takes a look at herself in the mirror. She knows what she sees, but still she beckons hubby to come and offer his opinion. "Hubby, does this dress make my butt look big?"

I always tell my coaching clients that if you have to ask that question, you already know the answer. Of course, wifey is able to see what hubby sees, and she knows that dress number ninety-nine makes her butt look enormous. Yet she expects hubby to tell her, "No, that looks just fine." And hubby knows that dress number ninety-nine makes wifey's butt look like the rear side of a cow, but he is wise. He knows what his response must be, no matter what.

Both hubby and wifey are disguising the truth in their own way, and they are comfortable with it because that's just how polite society behaves. Actually, it reminds me of the children's television show *Mr. Roger's Neighborhood*. In every episode, the host of the program, Mr. Rogers, would tell the young viewers it was time to go to the land of make believe. This was accomplished by following a red and yellow miniature streetcar, known as the Neighborhood Trolley, to the land of make believe. When the viewer arrived there, there were no adults, and all the characters were puppets.

In this fictional place, there was no sadness and everything was full of fun. The puppets were all exceptionally polite and very kind to each other. This was done to help the children who were watching to feel really good about themselves. After about five minutes, the trolley would return, and the viewer would have to leave the land of make believe. Well, the adult version of the land of make believe was initially introduced to modern culture as political correctness. Like many ideas, the original purpose was welcomed and well-intended. It was an opportunity to bring an appropriate awareness to those less fortunate and to discourage discrimination practices within our society.

Somewhere along the way, however, political correctness took on a life of its own and was applied to every conceivable area of our lives. Recently, I saw my neighbor, Missy, and her thirteen-year-old son, Luke, in the supermarket. Luke had on a sweaty soccer uniform with shin guards and cleats. It was readily apparent that he had just played in a soccer match. Making polite conversation, I asked Luke if his team had won the game. Suddenly, there was a look of shock and awe from his mother, and then Missy looked at me like a court prosecutor issuing an immediate cease and desist order.

In a very lame attempt to prevent Luke from hearing her, Missy whispered to me, "In Luke's soccer league they don't keep score. This way there isn't a clearly defined winner and, therefore, nobody loses." Oh, silly me, I thought sarcastically. Why would a group of thirteen-year-old boys have to face such harshness in their young lives? The possibility of losing a recreational soccer match would certainly prove far too traumatic for Luke and his team mates. As I walked away from this encounter, I couldn't help but wonder what ever happened to the life lessons that sports were supposed to teach us, namely the value of teamwork, the thrill of victory, losing graciously, and good sportsmanship.

> **ALL TRUTHS ARE EASY TO UNDERSTAND ONCE THEY ARE DISCOVERED; THE POINT IS TO DISCOVER THEM.**
>
> - GALILEO -

Then I realized that our society has morphed into a hybrid of denial and niceness that disguises itself as the new order of political correctness. We have become so conditioned to diluting the truth because that way we never really have to taste truth when it is served to us. People are so far from the truth that they don't even want their children to experience real life. They fear the children will learn that life isn't always going to be nice to them, and that's okay. Or they might realize that in life you won't always get your way, but with hard work you can always make a way; you win some and lose some, but the more important thing is to always do your best. What a paradox our modern culture has become. In the real world, we live in a suspended state of denial, but our number one form of escape and entertainment is based on reality.

Living in a world where denial trumps truth often times makes it challenging to recognize areas for change and / or improvement. *The Designer Life*, however, requires of you to give yourself the truth at all costs. The good news is that when you are dealing with yourself, there's no fear of being politically incorrect. Whatever you have to say won't be used against you but for you. Facing your truth will enable you to move forward in a direction that makes sense for who you are and where you want to go. Yes, I know there are times when the truth hurts, but it will set you free. Don't worry. It's okay if you offend yourself; it will be your launching pad for change.

As you seek to take your thoughts captive and begin the process of evaluating your life, I want to assure you that it's not as bad as it seems. Once you recognize the need for change and begin taking an honest look at yourself and your surroundings, try not to overdramatize the severity of the situation. If your life has been on cruise control for a long period of time, once you take over your life, there is a tendency to see it as much worse than it really is.

Picture a young child who is having a good time riding her bicycle. She thinks everything is just fine as she pedals along enjoying the ride, but then she falls off the bike. You see her fall, and you can quickly asses that, based on the slow speed she was travelling and the fact that she landed in the grass, there is no way she is hurt that badly. Yet the child is screaming and crying and flailing about like the accident is going to be fatal.

You are able to convince the child to calm down and that everything is going to be okay; the fall wasn't nearly as bad as she thinks it is. You see, this young child needs to let her brain catch up with the fact that while she did indeed fall, it's okay. She will be able to get back up and ride again. That is what you will have to do when you begin to see your life and realize that there may be some areas where you have fallen down, but don't just lie there screaming, crying, and flailing about. Recognize that it's not as bad as you think it is, and you will be able to get back up and ride again.

The difference between how bad things are and how bad we think they are is all a matter of perspective. I believe the best way to look at perspective is to personalize it, and think back in time to a situation that, at the time, appeared to have dire consequences. If you can, go back to something in your childhood or very young adult life.

It's amazing what perspective can do for a situation. My most telling example of clarity and perspective, or the lack thereof, is during my senior year of high school. I did not have a prom date for what I believed to be the most important night of my life. There wasn't anyone from school or my neighborhood or from among my brother's friends or the brothers of my friends who wanted to take me to the prom. I couldn't believe something like this could happen to me.

I had looked forward to my prom throughout high school. My dress had been selected six months in advance of the event. Hours had been spent poring through fashion magazines trying to find the right hairstyle. This was supposed to be a night to remember, but the closer it got to prom time, what I had anxiously anticipated for years had become the biggest source of stress for me and, unfortunately, for my family. Everything in my little young life revolved around not having a prom date.

You see, at that time I believed that my life was doomed, and I would forever live with the embarrassment, humiliation, and utter sadness of not being asked to what seemed like the most important occasion in my life. There was no way I could ever show my face in public because surely there had to be such a thing as dying of shame. Even if I didn't die of the shame, how would I ever move on with life knowing that I was such a failure? This is the type of ridiculous thought pattern I was faced with at the tender age of seventeen. I was not able to put the prom in its proper perspective.

Of course, as adults we are readily able to put something like a prom date, or the lack thereof, into the proper perspective. In fact, it's actually comical to think I was so dramatic about something so insignificant, but that's what perspective does. Without perspective, you can spiral out of control and believe the situation is far graver than it really is. Many years later, when I went to my high school reunion, I was able to laugh about not having a date for the prom. Even more entertaining was that several of my male classmates indicated that they assumed I had a date, so they didn't even bother asking me to the prom.

Fortunately, this was youthful folly, and nothing ever came of my ridiculous antics, but what happens when we don't have perspective as adults? Coaching clients have come to me believing they needed to make major decisions, such as career changes, marriage or divorce, all due to a lack of perspective. I would encourage you to take some time to consider the perspective you have of the current events in your life.

WE DON'T SEE THINGS AS THEY ARE; WE SEE THEM AS WE ARE.

- ANAÏS NIN -

There are things that might be causing you to feel sad, stressed, embarrassed or angry or that might just be occupying far too much of your time and energy. Perhaps it is a boss or a job you do not enjoy, a child who does not fit into your vision, a spouse that does not understand you, or financial lack for non-essential things. Are you managing your circumstance with perspective, or are you over-dramatizing your situation? As you begin *The Designer Life* it is important for you to put things in their proper perspective. The best advice I ever received on perspective came from my dad who said, "Anything in life that doesn't kill you only makes you stronger."

Your mindset, your thoughts, and your perspectives are all very important aspects to consider as you begin designing your life. I spent a great deal of time analyzing and learning about the importance of making positive changes in all areas of life. As I began to recognize what to improve upon, I came upon yet another important ingredient that must be added. It wasn't enough to just think positively, but I needed to hear positive words and speak positive words. There had to be a complete shift of everything. One without the other was like putting a Band-Aid on a bleeding wound; it might work for a temporary fix, but eventually, it would burst, and the problem would still be there.

The tricky part about whom and what we listen to is that, unlike our thoughts, it is not under our control at all times. Sometimes it is a boss or co-worker, and it is more challenging to steer him or her in a different direction. If people we must interact with are negative and focus on the negative, we will have to bolster ourselves to remain positive in their presence. It also requires the ability to use what I consider selective hearing. This is when you filter what you hear and, more importantly, what you listen to.

> **WE HAVE TWO EARS AND ONE MOUTH SO THAT WE CAN LISTEN TWICE AS MUCH AS WE SPEAK.**
>
> - EPICTETUS -

There is a difference between what you hear and what you listen to. If you are not sure how this works, try lecturing a teenager about something mundane like a clean room or a curfew. Don't worry; if you don't have a teenager in your home, ask any relative or even a neighbor, and he or she will gladly let you borrow one for a few hours. Begin to lecture the teen, and I can promise you that he or she has the physical ability to hear you. He or she will be aware that you are speaking and will recognize that there is an audible sound coming out of your mouth. But what he or she will not do is actually hear you by taking in anything you are saying. Teens have mastered the fine art of how to tune out and deploy selective hearing.

I have, however, noticed that many of my clients who want to design their lives say that the things they listen to are by choice. For some, the negativity comes from friends or family members whereas others get their negative hearing from television and / or radio. Of course, there are a few people who get their negative hearing from a combination of different venues. Unfortunately, there isn't any filtering process, and they willingly listen to and hear a wealth of negative commentary. Equally unfortunate is the fact that the things they choose to hear are actually counterproductive to their stated goals.

Several years ago, I worked with a client named Leah.

She decided to hire a life coach because she was very successful personally but felt that her social life was suffering miserably. When I first met Leah, she was the classic A-type over-achiever personality. Leah graduated from high school at sixteen years old, college at twenty years old, and completed law school at the top of her class by the age of twenty three years old. When Leah and I began working together, she was twenty eight years old, worked at a very prominent law firm, owned a beautiful home, and drove an exotic sports car.

Because Leah was very successful academically and professionally, she determined to be successful personally as well. She had already decided that her next frontier of accomplishment was marriage. Leah wanted to be married and have a baby before the age of thirty. She had two years to accomplish her goal and didn't want to waste any time. As I got to know Leah, I discovered that she loved hip-hop music. Rap music was her absolute favorite, and Leah told me about some of the artists she liked listening to.

Fortunately, I do my best to stay in touch with a cross section of pop culture, so I was very familiar with some of the performers she named. I asked Leah if she ever attended their concerts or purchased their music or whether she strictly listened to them on the radio. Of course she seemed a bit surprised by my probing in this area because, after all, she only wanted me to tell her step by step what she needed to improve upon to get a husband. Concert going and music purchases were inconsequential, or were they?

Leah informed me that she attended concerts and bought CD's all the time, so she could listen during her commute to work and while at the gym. "Very interesting," I thought. Being familiar with the music, I asked Leah why, if her goal was to become a wife, would she continually listen to music that called her a female dog and a garden tool? What seemed like pure entertainment was reinforcing negative images and stereotypes in her mind. How do you visualize and think about being a wife when you spend time listening to and sometimes even singing along to music that is belittling and demeaning?

I suggested to Leah that for at least a month she shouldn't listen to any hip-hop or rap music that had any profanity or negative stereotypes. Instead, she should replace her commute or gym time with either music that portrayed women in a positive light or some form of motivational and inspirational affirmations. It took a while, but eventually Leah admitted to me, and more importantly to herself, that she was surprised by the impact of listening to positive affirmations. Leah also informed me that once she stopped listening to "gangsta rap" it sounded very offensive to her when she heard it again months later.

Fast forward to the future, and Leah did get married. She recently sent me an email with a photo of her newborn baby boy. Leah explained to me that she felt very blessed to have the family she always wanted, even if she didn't meet her two year goal. She went on to say that as a mother, she didn't want her son exposed to music that perpetuates negative images of women. Leah informed me that she plays classical music and poetry readings in her son's nursery because she wants him to develop intellectual pursuits. Of course, when I read Leah's mail, I found humor in her approach, but at least she had learned to recognize the value of selective hearing.

Lifestyle Lessons

1. Perhaps you may notice a speck in someone else's eye, but usually the plank is in your own eye. The Designer Life change demands that you take ownership of the areas you need to improve upon.
2. We live in a society where denial can trump the truth, but facing your truth will enable you to move forward on the path of purpose.
3. Once you have inventoried your life, you must recognize that things are never as bad as they seem. The difference between how bad things are and how bad you think they are is all a matter of perspective.

Design This

Designing your life requires you to walk in the wisdom of your truth. You already know that the truth shall set you free, but embrace the fact that it is all about you -- your truth about your life.

CHAPTER THREE

> **KEEP COMPANY WITH GOOD MEN, AND YOU'LL INCREASE THEIR NUMBER.**
>
> - ITALIAN PROVERB -

Throughout my childhood, I remember my parents serving up nuggets of wisdom meant to instill values, prove a point, and generally make them seem wise and long-suffering. Dad would always say, "A mind is a terrible thing to waste" after he recounted walking in the ice and snow for many hours just to attend school. Mom would always say, "Cleanliness is next to godliness, and you want to get as close as you can" to illustrate the importance of a clean room.

I also noticed that when other adult relatives would gather, inevitably someone would recount an experience or tell a story and, like magic, a catchy phrase would appear at the end: "Pride comes before a fall." "God helps those who help themselves." "Beauty is only skin deep." "I paid the cost to be the boss." And whenever these catchy phrases were spoken, it was like putting an exclamation mark on whatever point was being made. All heads in the room would nod in unison and agreement. They understood that you could not dispute the story, and there was nothing more that needed to be said.

The problem is that for many of us, these catchy nuggets of wisdom didn't become relevant until many years later, often after we had already learned the lesson the hard way. One such adage I can remember is to be careful of the company you keep. When I heard it in my youth, it was to remind my mischievous brother that he should have friends who would not get him into trouble. I don't know if my parents ever recognized that my brother was actually the ring leader in his youthful pranks, and he was the company that he was keeping, but I'm sure at the time it sounded like the right thing to say, and they meant well.

A MAN IS KNOWN BY THE COMPANY HE KEEPS.

- ENGLISH PROVERB -

Interestingly enough, the states may be united in title, but culturally they are extremely separated by region. On New Year's Day, as I packed away the last of the Christmas decorations, I realized that I had become just like them. "Who are they?" you ask. They are southerners. I know my friends and family from the northeast are gasping right now, and some may even be on the verge of an anxiety attack. I have always been so proud of being from the northeast. Ten years ago when I moved south to what natives fondly refer to as the dirty dirty, I was determined to retain my northern identity. No twang talking and slow walking for this Yankee!

But my southern conversion all started with something as simple as decorating for Christmas. The first year I lived in Georgia I noticed that on the Friday after Thanksgiving my neighborhood was completely aglow with Christmas decorations. Then on New Year's Day, like it was the law of the land, people removed their decorations. Well okay, I thrive on competition and being my best. There was no way I was going to become the neighborhood slacker. Once I learned the rules of engagement, I vowed that the following year I would be one step ahead of the game. I would get my Christmas decorations up by the Wednesday before Thanksgiving, but my southernism didn't stop with the mistletoe and the garland.

I started doing things straight out of the handbook of *Southern Living*. When my carpool partner was sick, I made her family a hearty, meaty casserole. When new neighbors moved in, I baked them a butter-rich pound cake and told them to come by anytime if they needed anything. And whenever I made a pitcher of iced tea, I would put in a heaping helping of white refined sugar with some fresh mint leaves. As hard as I may have tried to avoid it, I had become indoctrinated into the southern way of doing things. It is difficult to pinpoint when my actual transformation occurred, but just being in the Deep South and living among the southerners had caused the change.

Isn't that just how life works? Eventually, the people we surround ourselves with, the situations we sustain, and the relationships we maintain begin to influence us. Over time, in a very slow and subtle way, we will adopt habits and behaviors that are indicative of the people and places we frequent. Like me, you may even vow to maintain your own identity, but it is human nature for our circumstances and our environment to become a part of the tapestry of our lives. That is why you have to be careful of the company you keep.

BECOME WISE BY WALKING WITH THE WISE; HANG OUT WITH FOOLS AND WATCH YOUR LIFE FALL TO PIECES.

- THE BOOK OF PROVERBS -

My experience with moving to the south was like the frog and the boiling water experiment. If you place a frog in a pan of boiling water, it will immediately jump out. But if you place a frog in cool water and very gradually turn up the heat, the frog will remain in the pan of water even after it has begun to boil. Initially, I moved to Georgia resistant to southern culture and determined not to adopt any of the habits. Very gradually, however, I began to let my environment influence me, and eventually it came to the point that I had become very much what I thought I wanted to avoid. The water started to boil, but because it happened over a period of time, I didn't even notice.

Fortunately, taking on the habits and culture of the southern part of the country is not in and of itself problematic, and it certainly does not derail any plans for *The Designer Life*; however, what happens when your environment and the company you keep are not conducive for what you want out of life? If you are not careful, you can begin to accept your environment and see no need to jump out of the water. The heat will gradually increase, yet you are not willing to do anything to change it. Eventually, you will find yourself residing in the ridiculous, and you won't even realize it. Worse still, you begin to consider it normal.

For many years, I have asked coaching clients at the beginning of our initial sessions to describe their environment. When I begin to ask probing questions that cause them to really think about their circumstances, they usually begin to recognize that they are residing in the ridiculous. It's only when they are forced to take a good look at their environment and even say things out loud that they see their surroundings as they truly are. Of course, for some people, their environment is imposed upon them in childhood and it takes time, exposure, and hard work to make changes. I am referring to people who have made the conscious, adult choice to surround themselves with people and places that are completely out of sync with what they want for their designer life.

People form a huge component of our environment. Where you live, work, and play are important, but it still comes down to the company you keep. Rags to riches millionaire Jim Rohn would contend in his seminars that "we become the combined average of the five people we associate with most." Mr. Rohn believed that the people you associate with are the ones who most likely reflect your bank account, your health, your career choices, your self-esteem, your habits (good and bad), your interests, your values and your goals.

I would encourage you to evaluate your life and see how true this statement really is. Create your own list of what I will call the fab five and see how you compare. Are you setting the standard, keeping the status quo, or pulling the average down? Do you love spending time with your fab five or do you simply tolerate the experience? In life, people that influence you are either pulling you up, pulling you down, or keeping you in neutral. It's up to you to determine what experiences you want to gain from your fab five.

If you are still not convinced that the company you keep plays a vital role in all aspects of your life, consider the book *Vital Friends* by Tom Rath, *New York Times* Bestselling Author. In his book Mr. Rath describes a female colleague who dated a professional, competitive wrestler. Whenever the wrestler was preparing for a match, he would need to add extra bulk to his body. He accomplished this with ice cream and pizza. And because they were dating, the female colleague ate pizza and ice cream right along with him. Unfortunately, the relationship ended, and Mr. Rath's colleague was fifteen pounds heavier.

When Mr. Rath's colleague shared her experience, it actually raised questions for him. He was fascinated at the concept and wanted to find out how common this was. Fortunately, Mr. Rath is an executive with the Gallup Organization, the largest surveyor of public opinion around the world. He decided to go looking for answers and had a Gallup poll conducted to find out about the impact of our influences. Mr. Rath learned that if your best friend has a very healthy diet, you are five times as likely to have a healthy diet yourself.

The second component of the study was that Mr.

Rath surveyed people about their best friend's level of physical activity. He looked closely at the group who had a best friend who was not physically active. Not one of them was very physically active either. As Mr. Rath puts it, "Even if these findings are confounded by other variables, it appears that your best friend might just shape you in a more literal way than you ever imagined." This just emphasizes the importance of being careful of the company you keep.

Hopefully, you are now aware and convinced that your environment and your fab five have a tremendous impact on you. Good or bad, we become a by-product of the people who are closest to us and the places where we spend most of our time. That being the case, what happens when the people within our circle of influence are actually hindering our goals and plans? As life would have it, sometimes these are the same people that we call family, friends, and loved ones.

THEY BRIBED AGENTS TO WORK AGAINST THEM AND FRUSTRATE THEIR PLANS.

- THE BOOK OF EZRA -

My husband and I often share riproaring laughter about my mother-in-law and what can best be described as warm negativity. Mom Speller is eighty-plus years old and a very sweet, endearing woman. Whenever she meets a stranger, she is always willing to share a kind word and a smile. She is just a very warm and gracious person, but as warm as her personality is, her bent towards worrying and negativity is second to none. She constantly looks for the worst possible outcome and is always prepared to help with what she perceives to be the impending doom, hence the phrase warm negativity that my husband has coined to describe his mother.

On any given day, a visit to Mom Speller's house will yield you incredible hospitality, served with a generous helping of hand wringing, head shaking and tsk-tsking. She will begin to speculate about what will happen when the bottom inevitably falls out of something or another, and then Mom Speller will usually do a roll call of her children and her grandchildren to see who needs the largest dose of her weekly worry. My son, Kyle, broke his thumb in a basketball scrimmage. When Grand-mom Speller found out about it, the ensuing conversation with her sounded a bit like this: "I'm so worried about my boy Kyle. They say once you break a bone, it never heals back the same. I hope he is still able to play, and he needs to be careful that arthritis doesn't set into his thumb."

The negative thoughts and questions were coming faster than a speeding train. I had to talk quickly to calm Mom Speller down and assure her that Kyle and his thumb would be fine, that modern medicine had made incredible advances in treating broken appendages, and that there was every reason to believe that Kyle's thumb would be as good as new. Those of us who know her and love her recognize that her warm negativity is well meaning, and it's because she cares. But even when we have well- meaning friends and relatives in our midst, if not managed properly and seen in the correct context, their presence can have very detrimental consequences.

Sherry was one of my coaching clients who had been a mortgage company executive. When the housing crisis first began in the United States, Sherry was one of the first employees to go. Fortunately, Sherry had established a lengthy career, and even though she was no longer employed, she did receive a very generous exit package. When Sherry and I began working together, she wanted to start her own business. Her dream had always been to one day become an entrepreneur, but the demands of her career had always prevented her from focusing on a start-up business.

When Sherry lost her job, she saw it as an opportunity for a new beginning. The problem was that her husband, her parents, and even her siblings, did not feel the same way. Sherry's loved ones wanted her to play it safe. They thought she should put her exit money into a conservative savings plan for retirement. Her parents thought she should look for another job within the industry, even if she had to accept a lesser salary. Her husband was a little more open minded and thought that a career change would be okay as long as it led to her going back to work and maintaining stability.

GOD HAS ENTRUSTED ME WITH MYSELF.

- EPICTETUS -

This created a real challenge for Sherry. Her circle of influence was very unsupportive of what she wanted to design for her life. Sherry was being bombarded with negative comments like, "It won't work out. You've never owned your own business before. Who starts a business in a recession?" Fortunately, Sherry was not deterred and was not willing to give up on her dream so easily. While it did bother her that she was not surrounded by a support system, she was determined to examine all her options.

As Sherry and I worked together, she began to recognize how much influence her family had had on her for most of her life. She realized that she had always been a people pleaser and would tend to not assert her desires if she felt they would not be well received with consent and / or approval. Sherry wanted to design her life and create the results that she desired regardless of what those around her thought. She wanted to exercise caution and good judgment with her decision making, but she didn't want to allow her life to be designed by the influences of her environment.

Several months after Sherry and I started working together, she began to realize that she could gradually transition her tendency towards people pleasing and become more of her own person. As she worked on her business plan, she constantly reminded herself that for over ten years she had successfully run a business; she just didn't own it. There was no reason for her to believe she was not capable of being an entrepreneur. I encouraged Sherry to deploy two of my basic principles. You are already familiar with the first principle, as described in Chapter Two, and have probably already mastered it, namely the fine art of selective hearing.

Sherry refused to feed into all the doubt and worst possible case scenarios her family presented. She resolved that, with selective hearing, she would only focus on the legitimate concerns that her family raised. Anything negative just for the sake of negativity was not worth the time and attention it would take to dispute it. The concerns of a start-up business in the midst of a recession did, however, seem like a legitimate position for her family to take. During one of our sessions, Sherry began having doubt in herself because it was obvious that the country was in a recession, and her family kept reminding her that she would be unwise to begin her business when the economy wasn't flourishing.

I suggested that Sherry do some research on Microsoft, Burger King, CNN, *Fortune Magazine*, and Hewlett Packard. What she discovered was that all these very successful companies were launched during a recession. How ironic that the world's largest global business publication, *Fortune Magazine*, was founded only four months after Wall Street crashed and marked the beginning of the Great Depression. The founders of Hewlett Packard began at the end of The Great Depression as an electronics company run out of a garage. In 2007, Hewlett Packard became the first technology company to exceed $100 billion in revenue. Now Sherry was able to silence her family's negative comments about the economy with tangible facts because documentation beats conversation any day of the week. She also realized that whenever you attempt to do something different, there will be naysayers who can create countless reasons why you should stay in the comfort zone with them. The Safety Susie's of the world will never venture into uncharted territory and do something different. Playing it safe is all they will ever know and do, but people who design their lives do their research and are prepared to make informed, calculated decisions regarding how and when they will come out of their comfort zones.

The second basic principle Sherry had to become familiar with is what I call managed expectations. Inevitably, there comes a time in life when we expect more and get less from people we are in relationship with, be it a spouse, a parent, a friend or even a co-worker. This happens when we project our expectations onto others and hold them to a standard that is not their own. Then when they do not act according to our standards, we are disappointed. Sherry expected her family to think as she thought and behave as she would have in the same situation. Had one of her loved ones been faced with the exact same circumstances as Sherry, she would have been supportive and encouraging of their goals.

What Sherry had to do was learn how to manage her expectations. Just because she had established a standard of behavior she would exhibit did not mean it applied to everyone else around her. Sherry needed to have realistic expectations of what was probable with her family, so she did not find herself in a constant state of the unlikely. It's like the old saying: "Treat everybody the way you would want to be treated." I prefer to treat everybody the way they want to be treated because we are all individuals and there is no cookie cutter approach for what we can expect from others. Even more importantly, it is not our job to decide the standards for others; we only have responsibility for ourselves.

THERE IS JUST ONE LIFE FOR EACH OF US: OUR OWN.

- EURIPIDES -

Another little nugget of wisdom I remember hearing in my childhood was not to follow the crowd. It was used to illustrate the importance of not doing something wrong just because others were doing it. For example, during my teenage years, some of my friends started experimenting with cigarettes. Of course, I knew that in this instance I shouldn't follow the crowd; however, I think we have to take it a step further and realize that sometimes we should not follow the crowd, not because they are doing something negative, but because they aren't doing anything at all. The crowd can become content with the status quo, and following them will get you more of the same.

Often, when someone like Sherry decides to stray from the pack and do things a little differently from what others feel is correct, it will either be met with criticism, or it will be greatly challenged. People will project their comfort zones into your life. Sometimes this behavior can have a positive effect and can challenge you as you develop and pursue your goals. At other times it can have a negative effect and can stunt your growth.

The important thing is to learn how to recognize and discern the different types of commentary, both spoken and implied. Some well-meaning forms of constructive criticism can challenge you to take a closer look at how you are managing your business and can even spur ideas to become more efficient and productive. The other form of criticism is merely a verbalization of someone else's fears. It really isn't about you and what you want to accomplish, but the negative they are sharing is bringing to light their shortcomings and doubts.

Sherry was going to gain much more by connecting

with people who were able to provide her with support and inspiration for her business endeavors because her family was unfortunately unable to provide positive reinforcement of her goals. Once she was able to accept their inability to play a supportive role in her goals, she could release herself to move forward in a way that was beneficial for her. The family members might have had good intentions and even concern for Sherry, but because of their own limitations, they were actually doing more harm than good.

As she launched her new business, Sherry joined her local chamber of commerce and a small business owner's association. This afforded her the opportunity to surround herself with individuals who shared her goal and her belief in business ownership. This becomes especially important when you have a circle of influence that can bombard you with doubt and fear. It's important to offset the negative with positive reassurance and encouragement. Business ownership, like most things in life, is not always going to be easy and without challenges. But whatever you desire to accomplish, you want people in your midst who understand your goals, can cheer you on, and who remind you that even though the road is sometimes bumpy, it will eventually smooth out.

A MAN ONLY LEARNS IN TWO WAYS, ONE BY READING, AND THE OTHER BY ASSOCIATION WITH SMARTER PEOPLE.

- WILL ROGERS -

A young woman sat at her table and complained to her mother that life was difficult and full of challenges. Her mother said nothing but merely got up and put three pots of water on the stove. In one pot, the mother put an egg, in another pot, she put a carrot, and in the third pot, she put a coffee bean. She let the pots boil for a time and then turned the stove off. The mother encouraged the daughter to come and examine the contents of the pots and what the boiling water had done.

She saw that the egg had gone into the water fragile and delicate with a fluid heart, but the boiling water had hardened the heart. The carrot went into the water hard and unbreakable, but the boiling water had made the carrot soft and limp. The coffee bean was unique. The boiling water didn't change the coffee bean, but the coffee bean had changed the water. As you begin to design your life and evaluate your environment and the company you keep, consider the egg, the carrot and the coffee bean.

The boiling water in this narrative represents life and its inherent environmental and circumstantial challenges. What I desire for you is to design your life like the coffee bean so that regardless of the situation and adversity you face, it won't change who you are and what you are destined to become. When tested with a challenging circumstance, just like the coffee bean, you can change the environment.

Lifestyle Lessons

1. The people you surround yourself with, the situations you sustain, and the relationships you maintain determine the course of your destiny and form the tapestry of your life.
2. You become a by-product of the people you spend the most time with, and your circle of influence is either pulling you up, pulling you down, or keeping you stuck where you are.
3. Designing your life requires the ability to step outside of your comfort zone, chart your own course, and pursue your purpose absent of the opinions and doubts of the company you keep.

Design This

When you begin to do something differently, your circle of influence will encourage you to remain the same. Some may even criticize you, but when you design your life, remember that criticism is simply the verbalization of someone else's fears.

CHAPTER FOUR

> **IN ALL YOUR WAYS ACKNOWLEDGE HIM AND HE WILL DIRECT YOUR PATHS.**
>
> - THE BOOK OF PROVERBS -

The beauty of *The Designer Life* is that it begins right where you are. You don't need to consult with your past to create your future. Where you started in life does not have to determine where you are going. I grew up in Philadelphia, Pennsylvania. My childhood was very interesting, and it was only as an adult that I realized the uniqueness and benefits of my formative years. I have a twin brother who is ten minutes older than I am. As children, our personalities couldn't have been more different, and now that we are adults the difference is even more apparent.

Our parents were as different from each other as my brother and I are. Dad is a very matter of fact, tell it like it is kind of guy. There are no frills about him, and what you see is what you get. He grew up in a very tough section of Philadelphia. He lied about his age to an army recruiter, and at the age of sixteen enlisted to go overseas and fight in World War II. While in the army, Dad learned to drink hard liquor and smoke cigarettes with the best of them.

Several years ago, when Dad was in the hospital recovering from an illness, the doctor was reviewing his medical chart and was astonished that Dad had been a heavy smoker for more than sixty years. I began to admonish Dad and asked what caused him to start smoking at such a young age. His response was, "What else was I going to do while I was sitting in a muddy foxhole in Germany, for days at a time, waiting for the enemy to come and try to kill me?" The answer was very typical of Dad: straight up, no chaser, directly to the point.

When Dad finished his tour of duty, he returned to Philadelphia and joined the police department. He enrolled in classes at night to complete his high school education. Dad's career as a police officer was well suited to his personality, and he was very successful. Eventually, his work was noticed by the police commissioner. He was promoted to a special forces homicide detective squad during a time when organized crime was running rampant, investigating and arresting crime bosses who are the legends of best-selling books and major motion pictures. It was also the catalyst for Dad to provide quite handsomely for his family.

LIFE ISN'T ABOUT FINDING YOURSELF, IT'S ABOUT CREATING YOURSELF.

- GEORGE BERNARD SHAW -

Mom's parents lived in a middle class neighborhood in Philadelphia, and she had a completely different experience. In middle school, mom went to live with her grandmother who was a grande dame of Philadelphia bourgeois society. My great-grandmother Lola instilled a sense of primness and properness into my mother that was second to none. Mom became quite the socialite at school and went to college after high school graduation. I can remember childhood visits with Granny, as we called her, wondering if she was real. Granny could sit rod-straight in a chair for hours, poised with her legs properly crossed at the ankles and her hands folded just so in her lap.

Mom is very talkative and extremely emotional, and because she is so focused on polite conversation, you will often find yourself wondering what the point is that she is trying to make. For my mother, appropriateness reigns supreme at all costs. What other people think matters, and social graces are worth their weight in gold. My mother took the lessons from her grandmother and quadrupled them into her own life.

Every aspect of my life is a by-product of two different worlds. In many families where the parents come from different backgrounds, there is more of a blending. Or one parent defers to the experiences, ideas and culture of the other parent, and together they create a more unified environment. Not so for our family. I had to learn at a very young age how to navigate in two very distinct worlds. The only common thread in our household was education. Both of my parents were sticklers for academic achievement. Dad was an educational zealot. He read incessantly and believed that education was the only way to success. Anything less than an A on a report card was considered unfavorable and unacceptable in our home.

Mom believed that one day I would need to take my rightful place in society, and she wanted to make sure I was prepared. My social résumé included debutante balls, being a prima ballerina, and membership in all the right social clubs. From the time I was five years old, I spent three days a week at ballet lessons and a full day of charm school on Saturdays. White Gloves and Party Manners was the name of my charm school, and for the life of me, I can't recall what I was learning every Saturday for almost ten years. What I do remember is having to wake early on Saturday mornings to put on a very fancy party dress with all the trimmings, including the requisite white gloves and shoes with a matching purse.

The charm school required its students to dress as if we were attending a fancy event at all times, so while other youngsters were in their pajamas watching cartoons and eating cold cereal, I was learning how to curtsey and what is considered appropriate behavior at high tea with the Queen of England. I'm not quite sure when it occurred to me that most of what I was learning in charm school didn't really have any practical application. I can't tell you the last time I curtseyed, and to date I have not had high tea with the Queen, but that is what was required to live in Mom's world.

For most of my childhood, Dad was undercover on his homicide assignments. This created a very interesting dynamic in our family. The safety and security measures we lived with seemed normal to me at the time, but as an adult it's hard for me to imagine living it. We had loaded guns everywhere in our home. We had big police revolvers and magnum 57's in the kitchen cabinet next to the plates, in the nightstand drawer, and even in the bathroom. I'm sure gun safety experts would cringe to know that children had access to loaded guns. In all honesty, I also find it difficult to understand, yet I lived it.

The best explanation I can offer is that because the guns were always a part of life, there wasn't any allure to play with them. Dad explained the guns and the harm they could do in explicit detail. They were not toys and were strictly for self-defense. He taught me how to load them and shoot them, but it was done is such a matter of fact manner that it never seemed like anything unusual. The guns to me were as miscellaneous as some of Dad's power tools in the garage. Sure I knew what an electric drill was and how it was used, but I had no desire to play with it. I felt the exact same way about Dad's guns.

Dad always stressed safety tips like making sure the house was completely dark when we went to bed at night. That way, if an intruder breeched the security system and got into the house, he would be disadvantaged because we knew the placement of furniture better than a stranger. So much for night lights. Some parents would remind their children to brush their teeth before going to bed, but Dad knew the dangers of his work, so before I went to bed, he would remind me that if a stranger got into the house and I had to shoot him, I had to shoot to kill. Any delay or hesitation on my part and the intruder would probably kill me. Talk about sweet dreams!

Preparation for proper society and social graces were the skills my mother emphasized, and the activities she required of me all helped toward that end. Street smarts, analytical skills and deductive reasoning skills were things my father emphasized. Dad thought one of the best ways for me to sharpen those skills was by evaluating very graphic and detailed clues in a murder case. Such was my life, a tale of two worlds.

> **LEAD A LIFE OF YOUR OWN DESIGN, ON YOUR OWN TERMS, NOT ONE OTHERS HAVE SCRIPTED FOR YOU.**
>
> - ANTHONY ROBBINS -

As hard as each of my parents tried to instill what they valued, it was still up to me to design my own life. Sure, the exposure and experiences in our youth can have an influence on whom we are, but they do not have to dictate where we are going. That is left completely up to us. *The Designer Life* requires that you know where you want to be, for if you know where you are going then it doesn't matter which way you go.

Several years ago, I read an article in the newspaper that declared the North Star and the North Pole as obsolete. We now have Global Positioning System, more commonly known as GPS. It is an unseen, mysterious force field telling us where we are and where we are going. GPS is managed by the United States Air Force 50th Space Wing and costs the U. S. government seven hundred and fifty million dollars per year.

I must admit that I love having GPS. I have a system in my car and an application on my mobile phone. In fact, for someone like me who has absolutely no sense of direction, GPS is a dream come true. Need to find a great restaurant, the closest movie theatre, or even a shopping mall? Then GPS is an excellent tool. As I read the article in the newspaper, though, I couldn't help but consider the deeper questions. For seven hundred and fifty million United States dollars every year, where are we really going? It is awfully nice that our social outings are aided by this magical directional system, but shouldn't we have more meaningful personal direction?

I wondered if the government was getting its money's worth with GPS. There are still so many people who don't know where they are going. Even with the existence of GPS, we still need an internal compass to determine the direction of our individual lives. No matter where or how your individual journey began, not even an expensive GPS can determine which way you are going.

I once attended a conference and met a young man who shared his story. His parents were both from the same rural community in the Jim Crow south. Both sets of grand-parents had been uneducated sharecroppers who lived hand to mouth. This young man had nothing but admiration as he described the boldness of his parents. They had married young, and both knew they wanted more out of life than what the small rural town could afford them. So the young couple set out to New York where they believed life offered more opportunities for black people – a place where hard work determined where you could go in life.

> **PEOPLE ARE ALWAYS BLAMING THEIR CIRCUMSTANCES FOR WHAT THEY ARE. I DON'T BELIEVE IN CIRCUMSTANCES. THE PEOPLE WHO GET ON IN THIS WORLD ARE THE PEOPLE WHO GET UP AND LOOK FOR THE CIRCUMSTANCES THEY WANT, AND, IF THEY CAN'T FIND THEM, MAKE THEM.**
>
> - GEORGE BERNARD SHAW -

The young couple soon discovered why the northeast is considered the concrete jungle because it truly is a survival of the fittest, and only the strong survive. Even though they were equipped with nothing more than the determination to succeed, the young couple began making a life in New York. Life was very difficult and the most their measly money would afford them was an apartment in a very dangerous public housing project, but where they lived wasn't nearly as important as where they wanted to go. They just continued to look toward the future their hard work would help them create.

This young man I met recounted in his story that even though he was born in a public housing project, his home life was happy and full of love. During his elementary years in school, however, the projects became an increasingly dangerous place. He joined a street gang at the age of eight years old, more because he had to and not because he wanted to. Gang affiliation was required if you wanted to survive on the streets. This young man describes being part of a gang initiation at the age of eleven. The gang leader, who was all of fourteen, wanted to prove how tough he was, so he shot his own father in cold blood.

The experience of the gang initiation was pivotal for the young man; he resolved he wanted a different life, so at a very young age, he began designing his life. He studied exceptionally hard in school and was at the top of his class. By high school, he had become an honor student and the president of his class. This young man's hard work was rewarded with a college scholarship, and he was grateful for the opportunity. When he attended college, he studied even harder and applied a double dose of the determination his parents had when they came to New York.

The young man remembered having a casual conversation in the kitchen with his parents during one of his college breaks when he told them, "I am going to be a multi-millionaire one day." He just knew it would happen and believed it with all of his heart. Fortunately, this young man had parents who had faith and who agreed with him that, yes, one day he would be a millionaire. After graduating from college, this young man entered the work force.

IF YOU DO NOT CHANGE DIRECTION, YOU MAY END UP WHERE YOU ARE HEADING.

- LAO TZU -

It wasn't long before the young man began to notice that technology was going to revolutionize the business world. Business machines were headed in a whole new direction, and he wanted to be a part of it, so the young man decided he wanted to learn about technology and further his education. He decided that a graduate degree was what he needed to really accomplish his goals. He worked during the day and went to school in the evenings to complete his Master's Degree.

Eventually, the young man went to work for a start-up computer company. He was a stellar employee who worked hard and played a pivotal role in the company's success. His efforts were rewarded with a hefty salary, profit sharing, and company stock. Twenty years earlier, when this young man told his parents he was going to become a multi-millionaire, he had no earthly idea how it was going to happen, but with faith, hard work and determination, this young man accomplished his goal while working at Dell Computer Corporation.

I didn't just have the good fortune to meet this young man and hear his story; I actually married him. I am certainly not sharing this to impress you, but to impress upon you the importance of determining your destiny. My husband, Bradie, and I are two people from completely different backgrounds, yet we ended up in the same place. If where you come from were the sole indicator of where you are going, Bradie and I would have never ended up in the same place. *The Designer Life* requires you to recognize and take responsibility for where you are going.

Perhaps it's easy to accept the concept that your past doesn't dictate your future and that where you were isn't nearly as important as where you are going. But what are you supposed to do if you aren't sure where you are going? You would do the very same thing you would do if you were driving along the road, and you were unclear as to which way you were going -- stop and get directions. Yes, it's just that simple.

I am often asked if people who hire coaches, go to seminars, or read self-help books are really that bad off. "Quite the contrary," is my typical response. You see, it's usually successful, self-aware people with a great deal of potential who seek assistance and direction. They know that asking questions and getting help isn't a sign of weakness but a sign of strength. Recognizing where you are and then deciding you want to be somewhere else is how you reach your destination.

THE BEST WAY TO PREDICT YOUR FUTURE IS TO CREATE IT.

- STEPHEN COVEY -

I recently read a study that indicated more Americans spend time planning their vacations than they spend planning their lives. This is a very interesting concept, and I have very loosely tested this theory by asking clients and audience members about their life plan. More often than not, they don't have one. Just in case you are wondering how people readily admit things to me, I make it easy to confess because I am so transparent about my triumphs and my tragedies. There was a time in the not so distant past that I didn't have a plan, and I readily admit it. Before I became consciously aware about designing my life, I was without direction, but like one of my favorite poets, Maya Angelou, says, "When you know better, you do better."

Imagine if you were going somewhere you had never been before. You would want to take the route that would ensure that you arrived at your destination in the most direct way possible. Having a plan is simply a method to capture the direction you would like to go. It doesn't need to be anything formal or complicated. But it does need to be well thought out and you should have pride in ownership. I would even recommend having a loose timeline associated with your plan because it creates personal accountability. I use the term loose because it doesn't need to specify the minute, the hour, or the day. It should, however, provide you with structure and something to aim for.

Once you have your plan and you know where you would like to go, I can't stress to you enough that your journey is as individual as you are. Stay focused on where you are going, and don't begin to compare where others are going or where they have already gone and how long it took them to get there. When my son, Kyle, was a baby, I constantly monitored his development based on what the average standard should be. The child development charts indicated that the average age for babies to begin crawling was about six months.

Well, six months came and went for Kyle, and he had not budged. He did not so much as even get on his hands and knees and look like he was going to crawl. Whenever we were with other children his age and they would begin to crawl, I would look at Kyle with hopeful anticipation, but he just sat there. Months went by, and Kyle continued to sit. I read parenting magazines and books by the socalled experts. Some said that crawling was critical in a child's development, and if a baby didn't crawl his sense of balance may be compromised, and he would lack strength in his hands and wrists. He could even be disadvantaged in things like holding a pencil, getting out of a swimming pool, or playing sports.

Then the milestone for walking approached. The developmental experts indicated that sometime around a year old, most children would walk. I would speak with other mothers, and they would gladly share their stories of how their little guy walked on his first birthday, some even at their birthday parties. Of course, I would meet the occasional over-zealous mothers who would revel in how young their child was when he or she had started walking. "Little Sally was only eight months old, and she was walking just as steady as you please," gushed one mother.

As Kyle's first birthday came and went, he continued to just sit. He still had not made any attempts to crawl. Walking seemed out of the question. He didn't even try to pull himself up while holding on to a table or a chair. Wherever I put him was exactly where he stayed. The pediatrician assured me Kyle was okay and that every child goes at his own pace.

At fourteen months old, I became concerned that Kyle still wasn't moving. He was a chubby baby, and I thought perhaps that impacted his ability to move. Perhaps the doctor had missed something when examining Kyle. I thought it was best for me to take Kyle in for a second opinion, so I scheduled an appointment with a pediatric orthopedic specialist. I reasoned that there must be a reason why my child didn't move, and I wanted to find out what it was. The specialist couldn't target anything specific that would prevent Kyle from moving. He basically sent me home with a pat on the back and told me to come back in a few months if there wasn't any change.

This was not exactly what I wanted to hear. I wanted answers as to why my little guy didn't move about, but it seemed that all I could do was wait and pray that Kyle was going to be okay. I continued taking him to play with other children his age, thinking that perhaps it might spur him to try and move about on his own. As we interacted with Kyle's peers, I watched the other children who were now not only crawling and walking, but some were even running. Kyle continued to be content to just sit and watch.

And watch is what I did. I compared how fast or how steadily other children could walk. I did mental calculations that if Kyle was this behind in crawling and walking, it would take years to catch up at the rate he was going. Seventeen months and two days after Kyle was born, he got up and walked across the room like he had been doing it all his life. His caretaker and I were in the family room of my home, and it just happened with no preamble to the big event. He just grabbed the end of the couch, stood up, took a few wobbly steps at first, and then started walking. I couldn't believe my eyes. I reached for the phone to call my husband and other family members. It had finally happened.

Fortunately, the experts are not the final word on a child's development. Even though Kyle never crawled, he never had any problems with pencils, or getting out of a swimming pool, or playing sports. The baby boy who took much longer than most to ever move has not stopped since his first steps. He was an all-star high school athlete and is now playing college basketball in the most competitive division in the country.

My experience with Kyle taught me a very valuable lesson that is beneficial for *The Designer Life*: everybody must begin to walk out his or her own journey at his or her own pace. Sure, there are certain milestones of accomplishment that can be standardized like the time frame to obtain a college degree, but for the most part, designing your life is not about comparison with someone else's life. It's about confidence in your own life. It's about being your best at all times, regardless of the time. Kyle may have begun walking differently than most, and later than most, but at the end of the day, he still walks just like everybody else. How and when he started have no bearing on how he will accomplish his goals.

Ironically, years after my husband, Bradie, and I were married, I met some of his high school friends. One friend in particular confessed that after they had graduated from college, they would take the train to Philadelphia, a short one-hour ride. They would do this in the hope of connecting with a "Philly girl" as we are commonly referred to. Someone had told Bradie that getting a Philly girl was the best, that they had it going on with beauty and brains. I'm not sure how true that is, but I'll take it!

Anyway, Bradie was determined, so he and this friend made numerous trips to Philadelphia, to no avail. No matter how hard he tried, there were no young ladies that connected with him. Then, in a small city in the opposite part of the country, Bradie met and married a Philly girl. As you design your life and think about where you started in life and where you are now, realize that everything that happened then was just the warm up act for everything that can happen when.

THE RACE IS NOT TO THE SWIFT NOR THE BATTLE TO THE STRONG.

- THE BOOK OF ECCLESIASTES -

I CAN'T CHANGE THE DIRECTION OF THE WIND BUT I CAN ADJUST MY SAILS TO ALWAYS REACH MY DESTINATION.

- JIMMY DEAN -

THE BEST WAY OUT IS ALWAYS THROUGH.

- ROBERT FROST -

Reflections

A bright future doesn't need permission from a dim past. Your life is a journey that can only best be travelled by you. Stay focused on where you want to go in life, and don't let anyone else determine your pace. Learn how to become comfortable arriving at your set time.

Lifestyle Lessons

1. The exposure and experiences of your youth can have an influence on who you are, but they do not need to dictate where you are going. Only you can determine destiny, but you have to design where you are going; otherwise, it won't matter which way you go.
2. When you don't know where you are going and appear to be lost, the simple solution is to stop what you are doing and ask for directions. People who seek self-help are not desperate; they are destined.
3. Your journey is as individual as you are. Stay focused on where you are going, and don't compare yourself to where other people are going or how long it took them to get there.

Design This

The Designer Life isn't about competing with someone else's life; it is all about having confidence in your own life. Know that where you started is just the beginning of an extraordinary and unique story that is waiting on you to write it.

CHAPTER FIVE

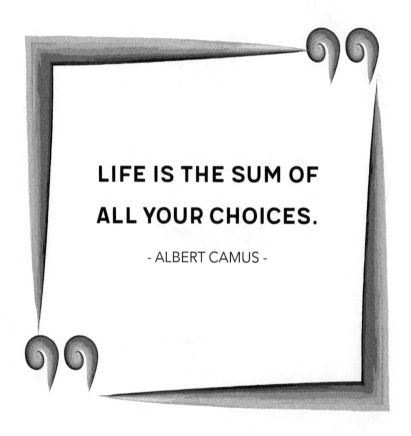

Just like where you started in life doesn't dictate where you are able to go, whom you are is not whom you must remain. Certainly, there are some attributes like gender, race, and age that are determined and established at birth, but everything else is all about the decisions we make. When I began designing my life, I began to recognize the impact of my decision making. Good, bad or indifferent, every decision could be traced to an outcome or circumstance in my life. Then I sought to understand the whole concept of choosing and what that looks like as it is applied in various situations.

The first thing I had to become crystal clear about was the difference between a choice and a decision. In some ways, we casually interchange the two words and don't really think much about them being very different. Interestingly enough, in a thesaurus, *decision* is considered synonymous with *choice*. But choice is not synonymous with decision. Hmm ... perhaps I spent a little too much time with murder mystery clues, but I thought there might be more to this and decided to do some further investigating.

I decided to tune into my own life and begin noting choices and decisions. You would be amazed at the discoveries made from observing the mundane things in life. It really is a matter of actually paying attention and turning off the cruise control. When my husband wants to go out for dinner and asks me if I want Japanese food or Mexican food, that is a choice. It is something presented to me for a selection. Baskin Robbins ice cream parlors pride themselves on having more than thirty-two flavors of ice cream. Walking into one of their stores always presents a wealth of choices, and even though there are many choices, when you pick a particular flavor of ice cream, it is also a selection.

Okay, so I was readily able to identify what choice is all about. It is simply a matter of selecting from any number of options presented to me. That's simple enough. My choices didn't seem to have much effect on my life as a whole. Restaurants and ice cream flavors are simple pleasures that, in the grand scheme of things, don't amount to much. So it must be the decisions that have more impact. I thought about how much I wrestled with the idea of actually doing work in Africa and spending time on the continent. By doing so, I would be limiting the time I had available to work in the United States. It would also mean time away from my family. Suddenly the stakes seemed a lot higher. That would require a decision. But ever the practical one, I needed a clear and concise way to define the difference.

It seemed to me that a choice was something presented

to me, but a decision was something that had a real impact on me. Choice was about possibilities and decision was about direction. A choice, like picking a flavor of ice cream, was what I would consider an until-we-meet-again selection. Whenever I returned to Baskin Robbins on a subsequent visit, I could simply make another choice; however, a decision can cut off or completely eliminate options. There may not be a chance to do it over again or make another selection. A decision brings conclusion to something. The stakes seem a lot higher in the decision category. A decision is, by its very definition, actually a turning point, a real game changer.

GOOD DECISIONS COME FROM EXPERIENCE, AND EXPERIENCE COMES FROM BAD DECISIONS.

- ANONYMOUS -

As I was paying close attention to the choice versus decision concept, I began to consider that some things call for a choice, and some things call for a decision, so what happens when we are doing one, but the circumstance clearly calls for the other? That is where things can become problematic. I have noticed clients who really struggle and are confused by this. I had to point out to them the importance of becoming clear about not only discerning the difference but applying the proper action for the proper situation. Decisions form our life path; they dictate the sum and substance of who we are, both personally and professionally. But choices and decisions are as individual as we all are. What may be a decision for you could be a choice to someone else, and nobody gets to decide that but you.

The important thing is to have enough self-awareness to identify what our selections mean for our lives. You don't want to avoid making good clear decisions because you are treating them like choices. You may be holding onto options that are holding you back. Conversely, you don't want to have anxiety and worry over every choice and treat it as a life changing decision. If you're wondering what this looks like in practical application, think of your friend who can't decide what to order from a dinner menu. She will sit and have anxiety as she factors in what she has a taste for, the portion size, the health benefits and if somebody else has ever had the same item. She is just completely over analyzing what is really a basic choice. My grandmother used to be the worst at menu selections. As she got older and went out for dinner, I would tell her, "Don't even worry about looking at the menu. The print is too small anyway." Then I would just order her some type of chicken dish because every American knows that when in doubt, chicken will help you out.

Then there are people who seem to be doing life by the seat of their pants. They move constantly, change jobs frequently, have career changes often, and sometimes have a divorce or two under their belt. Everything is simply a matter of choice. This person really doesn't make well-thought-out decisions. There isn't an analysis of potential outcomes or consequences. They just pick something and go with it, and if that wasn't the right choice, they pick again. *The Designer Life* should help you to create awareness around choices and decisions. It is very helpful to take a good look at the time and energy you are putting into the things that have life changing effects versus those that are just until we meet again. There is an expression that is common among people who play board games: "You study long, you study wrong." It is used to prompt an opponent not to take so long in choosing his next move. When it comes to choices, you could well apply the "you study long, you study wrong" approach because eventually you will probably get another chance. But since decisions affect direction, they need to be treated like you are invested in where the decisions will take you.

Because designing your life is as individual as you are, some areas of your life will be choices for you and decisions for others. Your values and goals will be strong indicators of how you go about the process of choosing and what your choices actually are. Fortunately, it is all subjective, and there is no right or wrong. It is just a matter of what works best for you and what helps you obtain the results you desire. The awesome thing about being an active participant in your life is that you become self-aware, and with that comes pride in ownership. Your life is your product; it's what is produced based on the sum of your choices and decisions.

Consider some areas of your life that are directly affected by what you choose to do or choose not to do. Physical health is one that many of my coaching clients and audience members have indicated they battle with. Most people now realize the benefits of healthy eating and exercise. Medical studies are published every other day informing us of the latest disease we can avoid if we quit smoking, lower our cholesterol, engage in moderate exercise, etc. General Motors America spends millions of dollars each year on their employee wellness program to encourage healthy eating and exercise. Other American corporations have discovered that paying for gym memberships for their employees is beneficial to the bottom line. People who have the opportunity to get regular exercise are less likely to get sick; therefore, productivity is improved.

IT IS OUR CHOICES THAT SHOW WHO WE TRULY ARE, FAR MORE THAN OUR ABILITIES.

- J K ROWLING -

Unless you have lived in a cave for the last ten years, you know the drill of what you should be doing. There really aren't any war secrets with the whole get-healthy-and-stay-healthy movement. Proponents remind us that it's all very simple; what you eat and what you do are like a hand in glove. When put together you will have a fit lifestyle. We are basically bombarded with the type of choices we should be making. I love listening to clients who can tell me chapter and verse what they already know they should be doing, but they just don't. They tell me they know they would feel better, they know they would have more energy, and they know they would have a better sense of wellbeing. I always remind them that knowing and doing are two separate and distinct places, and sometimes they don't even reside in the same street.

I am transparent enough to admit that one of my habits is lattes, and I use the word delicately. The deliciously decadent jolts of caffeine are incredibly addicting. In certain states in America, the law now requires of any business that sells food and or drinks to post the amount of fat and calories contained in every item on their menus. Suffice it to say that before the new law went into effect, I never gave much conscious thought to how many calories are in a mere cup of caffeine. But trust me, it is startling. In fact, I found it hard to differentiate between the calorie count and the price of my latte. As I looked at the menu board I found myself thinking that the 1,960 was perhaps a sudden price increase and not the intake of fat and calories. Was it possible for a latte to cost almost $2,000? Probably not.

Of course, I couldn't let this experience go by without asking the manager about this new policy. He informed me, "The purpose is to warn people about their choices, but it doesn't seem to change what people order." I pondered this for a few moments while I sipped on my latte. I realized that even though I noticed the outrageous number of calories, the warning did not deter me at all. Simply knowing did not affect my doing. Even though I tend to be very health conscious, I moved forward with my purchase anyway. I wondered if it was the same for smokers. The American Surgeon General has a warning that is stamped on every pack of cigarettes that is sold. For over twenty years, Americans have seen this warning that reminds them of the health dangers of smoking and nicotine, yet it does not seem to deter smokers. Could it be that we have become a culture that is desensitized to information that is supposed to help us make better choices? Perhaps we are so determined to keep doing what we have always done that we just keep on and hope for a better result.

Whether you make a decision or a choice, adopting a healthy lifestyle will certainly create benefits for achieving the results you desire. You want your designer life to reflect your personal best and whatever that looks like for you. It's not about a dress size or the size of your pants. Please let go of the imagery of what you see coming from Hollywood. The average actress in Los Angeles, California is a size two, but the average American woman is a size twelve. It seems like a slight disconnect! Then, some of what we see isn't even real. Think about how fabulous you could look if you had somebody photo shopping half of your dimply thigh out of a photo or airbrushing a six pack on top of your beer belly. The American media creates a lot of hype around what they consider the ideal or the standard, but you can ditch the perfect and be your best. It's about placing value on whom you are and what you want out of life — so much so that you are willing to choose healthy habits.

Even when we know a different choice could or should be made, there is still the disconnection between the knowing and the doing. As you design your life, you will want to begin connecting the dots between the knowing and the doing. To do this, you have to move feelings out of the way. I believe that operating by feelings can lead to failure. Often times the things we need to do most are not necessarily what we feel like doing. Most people don't feel like going the extra mile, or feel like staying up late to study for an advanced degree, or feel like putting in some overtime at work to get that promotion. The list could go for quite some time of what we typically don't feel like doing. When you are able to successfully make the connection between knowing and doing, then you are able to make choices based on what needs to be done, not what you feel like doing.

> **FIVE FROGS ARE SITTING ON A LOG. FOUR DECIDE TO JUMP OFF. HOW MANY ARE LEFT? ANSWER: FIVE. WHY? BECAUSE THERE'S A DIFFERENCE BETWEEN DECIDING AND DOING.**
>
> *- MARK FELDMAN AND MICHAEL SPRATT -*

I tell my clients that in life, it's not what we are doing that tires us most; it's the thought of things left undone. Picture yourself driving home from work in the afternoon. You had a good day at the office and all went well. Then you start thinking about helping your child with a school project, reviewing your presentation for work the next day, and having dinner with your spouse's boss. Now you are exhausted. You have thought yourself tired, and you don't feel like doing any one of the things on your list, let alone all three, but letting your feelings make the choice would not be wise. Each activity you need to do is important in your life. You must forget feeling and move into the decision realm. A good decision is one that eliminates the emotionalism and takes into account everything you know about the options you face – and then determining what you are going to do with the information. Both your choices and your decisions will be enhanced when you are able to actually marry what you know with what you do. The results will reflect a purposed life by design.

> **ATTITUDE IS A LITTLE THING THAT MAKES A BIG DIFFERENCE.**
>
> - SIR WINSTON CHURCHILL -

Our attitude is yet another area that is impacted by the choices and decisions we make. I am reminded of the elderly carpenter who was ready to retire. He told his employer, the contractor, of his plans to leave the house building business and live a more leisurely life with his wife and spend more time with his children and grandchildren. He knew he would miss receiving a steady pay check, but the carpenter was confident he had saved enough money and would be able to make ends meet. The contractor was sorry to see his best worker go and asked if he could build just one more house as a personal favor. The carpenter said yes, but in time it was easy to see that his heart was not in his work. His attitude was bad. He resorted to shoddy workmanship and used inferior materials. It was an unfortunate way to end a dedicated career. When the carpenter had finished his work, the employer came to inspect the house. Then he handed the front door key to the carpenter with the words, "This is your house. It is my gift to you." The carpenter was shocked. How could this be? What a shame! The carpenter felt that if only he had known he was building his own house, he would have done things so differently.

So it is with us. We build our lives a day at a time, often putting less than our best into the building. Then, with a shock, we realize that we are going to have to take up residence in the house that we have built. If we could do it all over again, we'd do it much differently, but, unfortunately, we cannot go back in time. When you design your life, you are the carpenter. Each day you hammer a nail, place a board, or erect a wall. Actually, your life is a do-it-yourself project. Just like the shows on television that take you step by step with what you could build in your home, the choices and decisions you make about your attitude today are building the house you will live in tomorrow; therefore, you want to build upon what you do and how you do it wisely because whatever you choose, it will become home.

My coaching experience has shown me that so many people govern their lives, make choices and decisions, based solely on what other people will think or how they will be perceived. I have worked with everyone from a dentist who wanted to be an elementary school teacher to an engineer who wanted to be a chef; their earlier decisions were made to please and / or impress other people. These are drastic examples of finding yourself in careers and circumstances that perhaps were not of your own choosing. But there are everyday examples of people who make choices with everybody, other than themselves, in mind. I recently watched a documentary that was examining the influence of the west on countries in the Middle East. It seems the effects are being seen in the increase of women choosing to undergo cosmetic surgery, especially in Saudi Arabia.

The reporter was reading statistics that showed that procedures for nose jobs, breast augmentation and liposuction, in that order, had seen significant increases in the last three years. Women in Saudi were catching up with their American counterparts and simply taking a scalpel to whatever bothered them. Now I am not against a little nip tuck if it helps people feel better about themselves, but what I found fascinating was that the women being interviewed all wore burqas, the traditional covering for Muslim women that only reveals their eyes. When the reporter asked the women about having plastic surgery and then covering up, they shrugged it off and thought nothing of it. Only their eyes are ever seen publicly, and at home only female relatives and a husband ever see them uncovered, but that had no bearing on having the cosmetic surgery. The Saudi women in the documentary simply decided to improve upon something that they felt needed to be changed. It didn't matter who would or who would not ever see the results. The decision to have surgery was made by these Saudi women even if they were the only people who would ever see the results. The choice was made because it represented what was important to them.
I immediately thought what a great way to go about

things. These women were very different from their counterparts in the west who had cosmetic surgery. There the improved, inflated, carved, suctioned body parts go on display for all the world to see. No discretion is needed in this country! The unwritten motto is, "if you paid for it, display it." I realized that some of my American clients could really learn something from the example set by the Saudi women – not necessarily post plastic surgery protocol, but on making a choice or a decision based upon what you value, what you want to accomplish, and what is important to you. For some, this approach could be revolutionary. Think about some of your choices in your own life, and consider those that were made strictly based on the outcome you desired as opposed to those made to incorporate the thoughts, opinions, and perceptions of others.

By giving permission to other people to influence your choices, you are actually abdicating the mere choice itself. Your decisions can't be done by proxy. Even if you make the wrong decision, it is better than not making the decision or making it for the wrong reasons. Design your life as if your choices would be covered by a burqa. Nobody would really ever see your choices, and your decisions would remain covered in public. They simply were made based on what you wanted and what was best for you.

IN ORDER TO DO WHAT YOU'VE NEVER DONE, YOU HAVE TO BE WHO YOU'VE NEVER BEEN.

- LES BROWN -

I am hopeful that you are beginning to have more clarity about your choices and your decisions and that you are able to recognize areas in your life where better choices can help propel you to where you want to be. Learning how to analyze your decision-making process equips you to make better choices and evaluate potential outcomes based on what you choose. Then you want to be competent in managing external influences to make sure you retain ownership of your choices. What I love about decisions is that they are constant, and even if one option is closed, other options will present themselves. Even though you can't go back in time and undo certain decisions, you can move forward with better decision making to create the life you desire.

Alfred Nobel was a Swedish chemist who invented dynamite, an invention he thought would be useful in ending world wars. When Alfred's brother, Ludvig, died, a French newspaper mistakenly ran an obituary for Alfred and called him "the merchant of death." Not wanting to go down in history with such a horrible epitaph, Mr. Nobel described the account as pivotal in his life. He decided that he wanted to be somebody who made the choice to create goodness with lasting value. Nobel set about to make his change, and when he died he left a will that shocked his relatives and the world for that matter. His will established the famous Nobel Prizes, of which the most notable is the Nobel Peace Prize. The first one was awarded in 1901, and they are still given out every year. The award consists of a gold medal and approximately 1.5 million dollars.

Just like Alfred Nobel, you can take a look at your life, and if there is something you don't like, you can be that person who made a choice to do something different. You are now aware of your ability to choose who and what you want to be, regardless of whom and what you were. What you do with this information is your choice … or your decision.

An American Indian fable tells the story of a Cherokee Indian describing to his grandson the battle that goes on inside of people. He said, "My son, the battle is between two wolves inside us all. One is an evil wolf. It is anger, envy, jealousy, sorrow, regret, greed, arrogance, self-pity, guilt, resentment, inferiority, lies, false pride, superiority and ego. The other is a good wolf.

It is joy, peace, love, hope, serenity, humility, kindness, benevolence, empathy, generosity, truth, compassion and faith."

The grandson thought about it for a minute and then asked his grandfather, "Which wolf wins?"

The old Cherokee grandfather simply replied, "The one you decide to feed."

Lifestyle Lessons

1. Your choices are about possibilities, and your decisions are about direction because a choice is presented to you, but a decision has an impact on you. Designing your life isn't about right or wrong, but it is all about options that shape your destiny.
2. Good decisions eliminate emotions and evaluate the possible outcomes. Recognize that information is your greatest asset and intelligence-based decisions are an investment in your future.
3. The choices you make and the decisions you face are as individual as you are and must be made based on the outcomes you desire and absent of the opinions and perceptions of other people.

Design This

Decisions are a constant, and even if one option is no longer available to you, other options will present themselves. While you can never go back in time and undo certain decisions, you can move forward with better decisions that will design the life you desire.

CHAPTER SIX

> **WE ARE NOT CREATURES OF CIRCUMSTANCE; WE ARE CREATORS OF CIRCUMSTANCE.**
>
> - BENJAMIN DISRAELI -

One of my favorite childhood memories is playing card games. Dad loved card games and taught my brother and me just about every game imaginable. It was not uncommon for Dad to have a deck of cards on the ready just about anywhere we would have down time together. Even at a restaurant we would place our order for food, and then Dad would pull out the cards, shuffle the deck, cut the cards, and begin dealing. It's funny to think that even at a very young age, I was extremely competitive and wanted to win. Some of the games we played were a matter of random luck based on the cards we received, but there was a game we played called pinochle that relied on concentration and skill as much as the cards that were dealt.

Whenever we played pinochle, if I were dealt what I perceived as a bad grouping of cards, I would complain. "This isn't a winning hand," or "I don't know how to strategize with such a lousy combination of cards," were my typical gripes. Dad, with his matter of fact style and intolerance for excuses, would respond with, "Play the hand you've been dealt." Then he would always take what seemed like a very basic activity like a card game and connect it to some important life lesson. Dad thrived on philosophy and wisdom, so there was always some life application in everything he discussed. There would be an explanation with examples that related to whatever point he was trying to make. In fact, when I was a very young girl, I thought the bronze statue in our home of *The Thinker* by Rodin was a miniature replica of my dad. It wasn't until I went to the Philadelphia Art Museum on an elementary school field trip that I realized it was actually a famous sculpture.

IT IS EASY TO MAKE EXCUSES WHEN WE OUGHT TO BE MAKING OPPORTUNITIES.

- WARREN WIERSBE -

Dad would begin to lecture that in life you sometimes do not get exactly what you think you want or need to be successful, but you have to make the most of what you have been given. Sitting back and complaining won't change anything, and eventually you will realize you just need to get on with things. This wasn't easy to hear at the tender age of ten. I really didn't see how my burning desire to beat my family in a card game had anything to do with what I was or wasn't going to get in life. I just wanted Dad to understand and sympathize with my plight, namely that I was faced with what seemed like insurmountable odds at winning based on the cards I had.

Another one of Dad's sucker-punch-to-the-gut expressions was about equality and fairness. Whenever I had experienced what I considered to be an extreme injustice, I would proceed to recount the event detail by detail, just waiting for Dad to be as outraged as I was or at least upset about the matter. Surely, he had to see that a grave wrong had been perpetuated that needed to be set right. For goodness sake, his career was based on seeing to it that justice was served and crime didn't go unpunished. This time just had to be the occasion for dad to understand my position, to sympathize with me, and perhaps even show me some pity. "That's not fair," I would boldly proclaim and wait for him to finally agree with me and see things my way. But without fail, time and time again, Dad would have the same response. Very calmly, with a shrug of his shoulders, he would tell me that life isn't fair and that whoever told me that it was fair had lied to me; the sooner I realized that life wasn't fair, the better off I would be.

In my years of coaching, I have encountered a good number of clients whom I wished I could offer an afternoon with my dad instead of a session with me. Coaching is great, but Dad's style would cut right to the heart of the matter. Perhaps it's because of the harsh life lessons that were delivered to me in my childhood with such candor and brutal honesty, or maybe it's a part of natural personality that has always been a part of who I am. Either way it goes, I am not very good at accepting obstacles and circumstances as an excuse not to move forward toward a desired outcome. In fact, in matters of parenting, I have often teased my husband, Bradie, that when our son, Kyle, was young, I usually felt like the bad cop, and he was usually the good cop. Bradie would always remind me that if you looked up the expression *tough love* in the dictionary, my photo would be next to the word *tough*, and his photo would be next to the word *love*.

THE ONLY PLACE WHERE SUCCESS COMES BEFORE WORK IS IN THE DICTIONARY.

- VINCE LOMBARDI -

The Designer Life requires you to adopt a military boot camp training mentality when it comes to getting *it* done in spite of. The *it* refers to your goals, and you can fill in the blank with whatever your desired outcome is. Regardless of what you seek to design, your will and your determination will be the defining factor in your success. How much of it you will need and how deep you will need to dig is all based on your individual style and approach to things. In fact, I have often noticed that clients with much greater challenges and more difficult circumstances will accomplish more than their counterparts with far less adverse conditions. I began to evaluate and analyze how some people are able to attain their goals and others just flounder around and talk about what they would like to see happen but never actualize anything.

As I looked for patterns that seemed to be key indicators of those that could and would and those that just didn't, I began to think in terms of athletics. In 1996, during the United States presidential elections, a phrase was coined to describe suburban American mothers who invested a lot of time with their children's sporting events. *Soccer mom* became a real buzz word and a persona was developed depicting this busy, minivan-driving, wonder woman. Well, some women may have been soccer moms, but I was super soccer mom. And while I drove a sport utility vehicle instead of a minivan, I would challenge any mom to a "who spent the most time and effort with youth sports?" contest.

So, in my role as soccer mom, every ounce of my competitive nature was channeled into whatever sport Kyle was playing. Typically, I would have Kyle and some of his team mates in my sports mobile when going to a game, and I would immediately begin giving the young guys their pep talk: "Go big or go home. The winner will always be who wants it the most. Leave it all on the court. Win or go home." And when they exited the car, my parting words were, "Now go get to work like you want the W." Was I over-zealous? Yes, of course. But there is something to be said about intensity when it accomplishes goals. I realized that there are common denominators in people who designed their lives and attained the outcomes they desired. They had passion, intensity, a can do attitude, and they did not make excuses based on circumstances or obstacles. These people were going big, leaving it on the court, and working like they wanted the W.

Most people face challenges and obstacles that stand between where they are and where they want to be. The difference is that people who design their lives and accomplish their goals have made the decision not to use circumstances as a crutch for their lack of accomplishment. I am reminded of the fable of "The King and the Boulder." One day a very wealthy king goes out into his kingdom with his servants and they place a huge, heavy boulder in the middle of the main road. The king then goes and hides behind a tree to observe. Merchants and trades people travelling along the road see the boulder and do nothing but complain about having to go out of their way to get around the boulder. They grumble at the inconvenience and think the king should do a better job keeping the roads clear. Then a peasant comes along carrying a heavy load. He approaches the boulder and puts his load down to try and move the boulder out of the way. After some time and a lot of struggle, the peasant is able to move the boulder to the side of the road. As he prepares to pick up his load and continue on his journey, he notices a purse that had been underneath the boulder. The peasant picks up the purse and looks inside to find untold wealth in the form of solid gold coins and a note from the king that says, "This gold is for the person who moves the boulder because he recognizes that what looks like an obstacle can become an opportunity."

THE WORLD IS ROUND AND THE PLACE WHICH MAY SEEM LIKE THE END MAY ALSO BE ONLY THE BEGINNING.

- IVY BAKER PRIEST -

As you are designing your life, it is important to acknowledge and identify your obstacles, but they should be viewed in the light of a possible solution, not a death sentence of your dreams and goals. One of the obstacles I hear quite often from clients and audience members is money. They have a perception that if they had more money, their problems would be solved. Then they could further their education, start a business, buy a home, or whatever it is they wanted to do. I hate being the bearer of bad news and having to snatch the rug out from under their excuses, but I have to give them the truth. And the truth of the matter is that money is not the problem at all. Actually, if money could solve all your problems, then your problems are not that grim. There are some challenges that even money cannot solve.

Look at Michael Jackson, arguably the greatest entertainer of our time. He was one of my favorites and the source of knock-down drag-out fights between my childhood friends and me. It was a real dilemma that there were four of us who thought we were going to grow up and marry Michael, but there was only one of him. Often we had to scratch and pull hair because one friend seemed to launch a more compelling argument that she was the soon to be Mrs. Michael Jackson. He was a real musical genius, a pop culture giant, and an international icon; however, at the time of his death, Michael Jackson was paying a doctor $100,000 per month to administer medicine to him, so he could simply get a good night's sleep. Now if money were the solution to the problem, how is it that Michael Jackson didn't have enough of it to resolve whatever problems he had that kept him from something as basic as sleeping?

Typically, when money is used as the obstacle, there is really another dynamic at work. It's easy and convenient to just wave the white flag of surrender at everything you want to accomplish and chalk it all up to finances. People respect money, so you don't lose any personal credibility when you speak of not moving forward because of a lack of finances. Instead of throwing in the towel, you have to be willing to set your goals and then decide how to best go about achieving them in spite of your current finances. Yes, it may be inconvenient, and you will want to blame others, just like in the fable, but in designing your life, you will have to see your obstacle, have a willingness to resolve it, and then discover the opportunities.

THE REAL MEASURE OF YOUR WEALTH IS HOW MUCH YOU'D BE WORTH IF YOU LOST ALL YOUR MONEY.

- ANONYMOUS -

When faced with identifying their challenges, most

people consider money to be their number one obstacle. But time or timing is a close second. I hear about it during coaching sessions, at workshops, and at seminars. Lengthy emails are sent giving me very detailed explanations that all reflect the issue of time. "There isn't enough time in the day. I'm just too busy. I would never have time to do that." These are some of the more common concerns that are presented when people are asked what is holding them back from attaining their goals. People will always make time for what matters most to them. The bottom line is that our lives reflect our values and interests. I've had clients keep a journal of daily activities, and at the end of a week, they are amazed at how they are really spending their time. It's an eye-opening activity to see in black and white how much time goes unaccounted for and is spent being unproductive.

Another aspect of time is the amount of time a particular task would take. By the time I finish that I will be (fill in the blank) years old, or it would take me (fill in the blank) number of years just to get that done. My response to that argument is to remind them that whether they design their life and pursue their goals or not, they will still be (fill in the blank) years old. So really, what difference does it make? The time it takes to accomplish what you want is going to pass whether you are actively working towards something or not.

The third aspect of time that is presented as an obstacle is timing. "This isn't the right time. I am waiting for this to happen before I can begin to work on that." The newsflash is that there is no set and appointed time to take ownership of your accomplishments. If you are waiting for the perfect time, you are in for a long wait, and you will find yourself in eternity still seeking that perfect time to get going with your goals.

The obstacle of "I've been knocked down before" is an interesting challenge for some people to move away from. If they have ever set a goal and didn't accomplish it or encountered some other obstacle, they can become paralyzed. Trying it again, or even trying something different, is too overwhelming. Perhaps they tried to move the boulder and were not successful with their first attempt, so in their mind it is just too big to move, and they just sit and complain about the difficulty of the task. Gary Richmond wrote a very interesting book entitled *The View From The Zoo*. In this book he describes the challenges of a baby giraffe. When a giraffe is born, it falls approximately 11 feet from its mother's womb and usually lands on its back, but within seconds it rolls over and tucks its legs in under its body.
Before the newborn calf can take it all in, the mother

giraffe very rudely introduces her offspring to the harsh reality of life. The mother giraffe lowers her head, long enough to take a quick look. Then she positions herself directly over her calf. She waits for about a minute, and then she does what seems like a very cruel thing. She swings her long, pendulous leg outward and kicks her baby so that it is sent sprawling head over heels. When the newborn calf doesn't get up, the violent process is repeated over and over again. The struggle for the calf to rise is momentous. As the baby calf grows tired, the mother kicks it again to stimulate its efforts. Finally, the calf stands for the first time on its wobbly legs. Then the mother giraffe does what at this point seems unthinkable: she kicks it off its feet again.

IT'S NOT WHETHER YOU GET KNOCKED DOWN; IT'S WHETHER YOU GET BACK UP.

- VINCE LOMBARDI -

At this point of reading the book, I found it hard to stomach that the gentle giants of the animal kingdom were so harsh on their young. Why, when the calf had just struggled so intently to get up, would she knock it right back down? As I continued reading, I realized it is because the mother giraffe wants the calf to remember how it got up. In the wild, baby giraffes must be able to get up as quickly as possible to stay with the herd where there is safety. Lions, hyenas, leopards and wild hunting dogs all enjoy young giraffes, and they would be easy prey if the mother didn't teach her calf to get up very quickly and get with it.

Who would have thought that there is something to be learned from the experiences of a baby giraffe? Getting knocked down and having to struggle to get back up can often be for our own good. The lessons we learn and the fortitude it takes to get back up can be just what we needed to learn to ensure our own survival. The famous American author Irving Stone understood this principle. He spent a lifetime studying greatness and penned biographies of men like Michelangelo, Vincent van Gogh and Sigmund Freud. Stone was once interviewed and asked what he saw as the common thread that runs through the lives of these exceptional people.

He said, "I write about people who sometime in their life have a vision or dream of something they should accomplish. They are beaten over the head, knocked down, and for years they get nowhere. But every time they are knocked down they stand up. You cannot destroy these people and at the end of their lives they accomplish what they set out to do." So instead of seeing what didn't work out the first time as an obstacle, see it as part of your process. Then struggle and fight to get back up, and try it again.

> **I NEVER KNEW A MAN THAT WAS GOOD AT MAKING EXCUSES WHO WAS GOOD AT ANYTHING ELSE.**
>
> - BENJAMIN FRANKLIN -

Try as I might to think of a polite way to address the obstacles that we all face in some form or another, I am unable to see them as anything else than excuses. Oops … I just used the very politically incorrect, dreaded word nobody wants to hear. By definition, an excuse is an explanation offered to justify or obtain forgiveness, but when it comes to designing your life, there isn't any justification, and there isn't anybody to seek forgiveness from because robbing yourself of the satisfaction of accomplishing your goals is really inexcusable.

Circumstances are different from obstacles because often times they are beyond our control. And certainly there are people with very difficult backgrounds and present day circumstances who are not using excuses as their crutch, but they have very real situations. Gender, race and family background can all be part of our circumstance. When faced with circumstance, the "in spite of," not the "because of," attitude becomes critical. You will need to make the decision to succeed in spite of any number of things you have faced or currently face. The important thing is to remain positive and not let yourself sink into the depths of despair because of your challenges.

> **THE ONLY DIFFERENCE BETWEEN A RUT AND A GRAVE IS THE DEPTH.**
>
> - ELLEN GLASGOW -

Your conversations with yourself should sound something like this: "I will graduate from college in spite of." Not, "Because of being born in public housing, I won't be able to attend college." "I will become the president of the company in spite of being a woman from a disadvantaged family." Not, "Because of being a woman from a disadvantaged family, I won't become president of the company." Practice speaking affirmations to yourself that declare what you will accomplish in spite of your circumstances. Think in terms of "If not me, then who? If not now, then when?" Instead of accepting your circumstance, challenge it. Decide that you may not be able to change the circumstance, but you can and will create the outcome of whatever your circumstance is.

Wilma Rudolph was the twentieth of twenty-two children. She was born prematurely, in the Jim Crow South, and her survival was doubtful. When she was four years old, she contracted double pneumonia and scarlet fever, which left her with a paralyzed left leg. At the age of nine, she removed the metal leg brace she had been dependent on and began to walk without it. By thirteen, she had developed a rhythmic walk, which doctors said was a miracle. That same year, she decided to become a runner. She entered a race and came in last. For the next few years, in every race she entered, she came in last. Everyone told her to quit, but she kept on running. One day, she actually won a race and then another. From then on, she won every race she entered. Eventually, this little girl, who was told she would never walk again, went on to win three Olympic gold medals in track and field for the United States. Ms. Rudolph made a decision that, regardless of how challenging her circumstance was, she was going to create the outcome she wanted, in spite of.

Isn't it amazing how much smarter your parents can become when you get older? When I became an adult, life began to happen to me as it happens to most of us. Suddenly, Dad's perspectives became invaluable. I realized that while I may have wanted sympathy and understanding as a child, what I got instead has served me over time and not just for a moment in time. The lessons we learn that can sustain us throughout life are actually priceless. Whenever I feel that an injustice has been done to me, I don't focus on feeling sorry for myself because I already know that life isn't fair, and the sooner I work on a resolution, the better off I'll be. I realize that I can't be powerful and pitiful at the same time, and I choose power not pity. Whenever I have wanted or needed to accomplish something but didn't have everything exactly as I needed it, or I felt like I was faced with insurmountable odds to be successful, I simply have played the hand I was dealt.

When I went back to school to become trained and certified as a life coach, I read a book by Dr. Viktor Emil Frankl entitled *Man's Search For Meaning*. Dr. Frankl was a professor of neurology and psychiatry at the University of Vienna. He was also a visiting professor at Harvard University. *The American Journal of Medicine* states, "His work is the most significant thinking since Freud." In *Man's Search For Meaning*, Dr. Frankl shares his horrific experiences at Auschwitz concentration camp: the dehumanizing conditions, being reduced to a number, and not knowing the fate of loved ones. From a psychological perspective, he discusses the ways in which the different prisoners reacted to their imprisonment, the challenges they each faced, and the way different people went about handling their circumstance. My favorite quote from this book is how Dr. Frankl saw his circumstance: "What was really needed was a fundamental change in our attitude toward life. We had to learn ourselves and, furthermore, we had to teach the despairing men, that it did not really matter what we expected from life, but rather what life expected from us."

Lifestyle Lessons

1. Sometimes life is unfair, and the temptation is to feel justified in our displeasure, but complaining about everything distracts you from changing anything. Wisdom requires that you make the most out of what you have to work with.
2. When designing your life, your will and determination will be the defining factors in your success. Determination will outlast your critics because success is a process, and every step of progress puts you closer toward your goal. Your determination will make up the difference for what you may lack in experience.
3. There are common denominators in people who design their lives and attain the outcomes they desire. They have passion, intensity, a cando attitude, and do not make excuses based on circumstances or obstacles.

Design This

Excuses are usually an unwanted explanation for being unprepared, and obstacles must be viewed in light of solutions, not a death sentence of your dreams and goals. Designing your life requires you to acknowledge your obstacles while seizing the opportunity to overcome them.

CHAPTER SEVEN

> IN ANY MOMENT OF DECISION
> THE BEST THING YOU CAN DO
> IS THE RIGHT THING, THE NEXT
> BEST THING IS THE WRONG
> THING, AND THE WORST THING
> YOU CAN DO IS NOTHING.
>
> - THEODORE ROOSEVELT -

People have always been my passion. Meeting new people and learning about different cultures and experiences have always been enjoyable to me. I love to ask questions, and I am always willing to answer questions. The more I know, the more I want to know, but not for the reasons some might think. Interacting with people and learning all about them is not because I am a nosy busybody with nothing better to do. It's because I consider it my research, just like a scientist who is looking for discoveries that will improve the lives of others. The difference is that I don't sit in a laboratory with test equipment; my laboratory is the general public.

One such discovery I have noted in the last few years is the power of resourcefulness. People who are resourceful and work with what they have tend to fare much better than their counterparts. Having interacted with a wealth of different types of people with varying backgrounds, I have seen the value of people who will try to get it done at all costs. Education and the ensuing degrees are proof that someone is capable of learning a particular subject matter, but resourcefulness speaks of a willingness to do what needs to be done with what you know and to find out more if you don't know. I have had coaching clients within an organization who had similar résumés of experience and education, but the one with exemplary resourcefulness skills was usually the one who succeeded with the task at hand.

Atlanta, Georgia, is located in what is considered the deep south of America. The weather in Georgia is pretty predictable for the most part. The heat and humidity begin in April and last until October. Natives fondly refer to the city as Hotlanta because the summer temperatures are so oppressive. Most homes are equipped with central air conditioning systems that run day and night for about five months of the year. Compared with other parts of the country, the winter season is very mild in Atlanta. Rarely does the temperature drop to freezing point, and winter days are typically cool, sunny and dry.

Well, like most things in life, there is an exception to every rule, and Atlanta recently experienced a huge exception to the rule – snow. Approximately three inches of the powdery white stuff fell out of the sky and blanketed the city. Coupled with freezing temperatures, the storm literally crippled Atlanta and brought everything to a standstill. Atlanta is home to the busiest airport as it moves more people per year than any other airport in the world. That title didn't mean anything when the snow came. Thousands of flights were cancelled, and people from around the globe were stranded. Banks and supermarkets were closed for days. Schools were dismissed for over a week. The breaking news on local television for more than seventy-two hours was the fact that it had actually snowed in Hotlanta. Meteorologists were doing their research to proclaim the blizzard of 2011 as the worst storm that had ever affected Georgia.

Having grown up in the northeast part of the country, snow was a very regular winter occurrence. We didn't dream about having a White Christmas; we lived it. In fact, for most U. S. cities that are accustomed to snow, the three inches Atlanta received would be laughable. At most, that amount of snow would have delayed the start of school by a few hours simply to allow time for the snow ploughs. The challenge with the snowfall in Atlanta was the lack of preparedness. The city doesn't really have snow removal equipment, and most households don't have a sturdy shovel or any of the other supplies typically found in homes where snow is an expected part of winter.

Once the snow settled, people began to face the day with their new reality. News reporters braved the elements to bring live coverage of the storm. Wanting to capture eye witness reports and human interest stories, camera crews were all over the city. One woman I saw interviewed was actually standing in her driveway, reduced to tears. She had never been in a snow storm and didn't know what to expect or what she should do. Yet another woman was interviewed, and she was shown in her garage proudly displaying the amount of food supplies she had purchased the day before the snow. Unless she had a small army holed up inside her home, the woman had enough canned goods to last seven months, not seven days.

In my neighborhood, several of the residents organized themselves to determine a way to conquer the snow. They took the mounds of white beach sand that is used for the golf course and dumped it on the main street. This was done in an attempt to create enough traction for a vehicle to safely navigate on the road. In another neighborhood, several people had gathered with garden rakes to try to clear a path in the snow. The Atlanta news channels were showing photos of people trying all types of methods to deal with the snow.

NECESSITY ... THE MOTHER OF INVENTION.

- PLATO -

One man was shown pouring fine table salt on his driveway. Another man was shown trying to move the snow with a makeshift shovel that was nothing more than his household broom with a plastic dustpan tied to the bottom. Still another person was bending down with a dustpan and a paint scraper trying to move the snow. These photos depicting Georgians and their various attempts at snow management began circulating to other parts of the country. In cities where massive amounts of snow are a regular occurrence, the photos were dubbed hilarious. Blog writers began to write jokes, and emails were sent out with all types of catchy phrases intended to make fun of the southerners who couldn't handle a little snow.

As I sat in my laboratory taking it all in, I had a completely different approach than the media and the blogosphere. I thought it was admirable that people were willing to do something to resolve their situation. They may have been ill-equipped, and their methods may not have been what are traditionally used for snow removal, but still, in all, these people were using what they had rather than sitting back doing nothing and waiting for something to change or waiting for somebody else to help. These pioneers decided to take matters in their own hands and to work with whatever tools they had available to them. Sure, any snow-savvy person realizes that coarse rock salt is more effective than table salt, and a sturdy metal shovel is what people typically use for snow removal, but what the locals did in an unfamiliar situation should be applauded. They recognized that even if you don't have the best of what you need, do your best with what you do have. There is no point in letting the good get in the way of the perfect.

The initiative, creativity, and resourcefulness demonstrated during Atlanta's blizzard of 2011 are principles that will serve you well as you design your life. It can be quite easy to sit back and do nothing because you believe there isn't anything you can do about your situation. Or maybe you perceive that your tools and / or resources are inadequate and insufficient to make a difference. Perhaps you have thought about trying to work with what you have but are concerned you may be ridiculed or become the laughing stock of your family and friends. Consider the people in Atlanta who showed the benefit of innovation and the value of focusing on what they had available to work with. These can-doers didn't throw a pity party because they were faced with something different and weren't quite sure how to manage it. Even though their pictures were on the news, and they became the subject of internet jokes, it didn't matter because they were focused on what they wanted to accomplish.

The Designer Life will require you to take stock of all the options that are available to you and to work with what's in your hand to bring about the results you desire in life. You have to focus on what can be done with whatever it is that you have. There will always be better tools and resources that exist somewhere in the world, but when you spend valuable time and energy thinking about what you don't have, you may miss the chance to stretch out your arm and use what is in your hand. Once in a lifetime opportunities only come once in the lifetime of that opportunity. When all you can see is what you don't have, you could miss your moment because you are not making the best of what you do have.

THEN THE LORD ASKED HIM WHAT'S THAT IN YOUR HAND?

- THE BOOK OF EXODUS -

When I am doing either individual or group coaching, I often encounter clients who will simply not utilize what they have. They are talented individuals who possess everything they need to accomplish their goals and what they indicate as important to them, yet there is something that will cause them to sit on their resources and capabilities. These people must discover what is holding them back from using everything available to them in their toolbox. Yes, it is vitally important to do so because if you don't use it, eventually you may lose it. Several years ago, I was speaking at a conference in the state of Michigan. It was sometime during the middle of February when winter was in full effect. Unlike Georgia, Michigan specializes in snow, ice and below freezing point temperatures. There was a story in the news regarding an elderly Michigan man who froze to death in his home when his gas heating service was disconnected due to an unpaid utility bill. As I sat and listened to the news report, I was initially saddened by the tragedy of it all, but that emotion was quickly replaced by anger. Actually, I was outraged that in a country as rich as America the elderly were dying in their homes needlessly because of something as basic as heat.

Activism is at the core of who I am. My family has often joked that it is a pity I am too young to have been part of the American civil rights movement. They say the struggle might have been completed in half the time because opponents would have been worn down by my relentlessness! If there is a cause I feel strongly about, I have been known to picket, demonstrate, march, or whatever else is needed to remedy an injustice. On my college campus, I was the leader of our school's anti-apartheid movement and organized all types of activities designed to force American corporations to divest in South Africa until the government changed its practices. As an adult, I championed for legislation to offer drug treatment to repeat criminal offenders with drug and alcohol arrests. For a fraction of the costs it took to incarcerate someone, you could provide detoxification and drug treatment to end the cycle of recidivism.

There have even been a few occasions when I was travelling internationally, and I would strongly disagree with a particular stance. My immediate reaction was that I should get to work organizing and launching a protest. My hosts would have to remind me what country I was in and that my over-zealous American approach would not work there. Standing up for the truth and advocating for justice are things I feel very strongly about, so I wrote a scathing letter to the utility company admonishing them for what happened to this poor man and requesting an investigation into how something like this could happen. I sent the letter to the gas company and then contacted the editor of the local Michigan newspaper for them to print my letter in the editorial section.

Like so many things in life, everything is not always as it seems. It turned out that the elderly man had not paid his utility bill for over a year. The gas company was trying to work with him, but he kept demanding to only pay the senior citizen fixed income rates for his gas service. This man was digging his heels in and stubbornly proclaimed he would not pay his bill unless he received the discount. The problem was that in order to qualify for the senior discount you had to be over the age of 65, have an income below a certain amount, have no more than $1,000 in a savings account, and have no other assets.

DON'T FIND FAULT. FIND A REMEDY.

- HENRY FORD -

The elderly man in Michigan had over $500,000 in the bank and assets worth more than $1,000,000.00. He didn't have any mental health challenges or disabilities. He simply refused to use his resources. Because I had brought the issue to such attention in the media, the gas company had to protect its image in the court of public opinion. Their attorney held a press conference and indicated that it was unfortunate this elderly gentleman made the choice not to utilize his resources for the benefit and sustainability of his own life. Equally as unfortunate, the money and assets would go to the state of Michigan since he died without a will and did not have any known living relatives. As sad as this story was, I began to consider the life lesson buried within.

So many people don't utilize their resources for their own good. They wander through life with skills, abilities and resources that remain untapped. Gifts and talents that should be used to sustain them and advance their purpose remain idle and often just fade away. I have met clients who refuse to act on their capabilities and thus risk being disconnected from their greatest blessing. Just like the unpaid utility bill of the elderly man who wanted others to believe he was limited due to his age or his income, they rationalize their actions or lack thereof and make excuses without considering the resources and assets that already exist. As you are designing your life, embrace your God-given gifts and talents and use them to benefit and sustain your own life.

Working with what's in your hand and utilizing everything at your disposal may require you to step outside your comfort zone and collaborate with others. Sometimes your tools and resources are tangible things, sometimes they are abilities, and sometimes they are found in other people. Your job is to learn how to recognize areas of strength in others and how they can help you improve upon some things. You also want to discover the benefits of working with others. I should caution you that the people who can add value to your experience are not always the ones that are just like you. Often times it is the people who are the least like you who can enhance an area in your life or add another tool to your toolbox.

Remember the age old fable of the tortoise and the hare race? Everyone knows who won the race, or do you? There is actually a more modern version of this fable that I would like you to consider. Once upon a time a tortoise and a hare had an argument about who was faster. They decided to settle the argument with a race. The tortoise and hare both agreed on a route and began the race. The hare shot ahead and ran briskly for some time. Then, seeing that he was far ahead of the tortoise, he thought he'd sit under a tree for some time and relax before continuing the race. He sat under the tree and soon fell asleep. The tortoise, plodding on, overtook him and soon finished the race, emerging as the undisputed champ. The hare woke up and realized that he'd lost the race. The moral of the story is that slow and steady wins the race.

But the story doesn't end there. You see, the hare was disappointed at losing the race, and he did some soul searching. He realized that he'd lost the race only because he had been over-confident, careless, and lax. If he had not taken his abilities for granted, there was no way the tortoise could have beaten him, so he challenged the tortoise to another race. The tortoise agreed. This time the hare went all out and ran without stopping from start to finish. He won by a mile.

Then the tortoise did some thinking and realized there was no way he could beat the hare in a race the way it was currently formatted. He thought about it for a while and then challenged the hare to another race but with a slightly different route. The hare agreed, so the tortoise and the hare started off again. In keeping with his commitment to be consistently fast, the hare took off and ran at top speed until he came to a broad river. The finish line for the race was a couple of miles on the other side of the river. The hare sat there wondering what to do. In the meantime, the tortoise came along, got into the river, swam to the opposite side, and reached the finish line to win the race.

At this point, the tortoise and the hare had become acquaintances and did some thinking together. They both realized that the race could be even better if they worked together, so they started off again. This time the hare carried the tortoise to the riverbank. There the tortoise took over and swam across with the hare on his back. On the other side of the river, the hare carried the tortoise again until they reached the finish line in record time. Now both the tortoise and the hare had a sense of satisfaction and accomplishment.

There are several morals of this story, and all of them are beneficial to designing the life that you desire. What I love the most about this modern twist to the fable is that neither the tortoise nor the hare gave up when they lost. They were both willing to examine what they could do differently, and they prepared to either work harder or change their strategy in order to work with what they had. This is a critical concept to remember because sometimes you actually have to work even harder than you expected with what's in your hand. But there are other times when what's in your hand isn't the tool for the job at hand, and you have to change your approach and develop a different solution altogether. Then there are times when you may have to do a little of both.

> **BECAUSE IF YOU'RE NOT GROWING YOU'RE DYING.**
>
> - LOU HOLTZ -

The other concept in this story that provides a framework

to learn from is that individual competency is great. Yes, designing your life is not, in and of itself, a group activity, but no man is an island. When you can work with someone who is strong in areas where you are weak, it affords you the opportunity for growth. Being able to see how someone else works toward something may show you an approach or a style that perhaps you hadn't even considered. This is not to say that you have to become a carbon copy of someone else or duplicate his or her methods with an exact science. It is merely to suggest that sometimes you don't have to reinvent the wheel; you just need to rotate the tires a bit. Change things around to accommodate where you are and where you want to go.

Lastly, consider that the tortoise and the hare originally put all their effort into competing against a perceived rival, each other. Sometimes another person is not your rival; it's the situation that is your rival. When Roberto Goizueta took over as the CEO of Coca-Cola in the 1980's, he was faced with intense competition from Pepsi that was eating into Coke's growth. The executives at Pepsi focused on increasing their market share against Coke one percent at a time. Goizueta decided that he wasn't going to compete against Pepsi, but was instead going to compete against the situation of one percent growth. He asked his Coke executives what the average fluid intake was of an American per day and found out it was about fourteen ounces. Coke's share of that was two ounces.

Goizueta contended that Coke needed a larger share of the market. Pepsi wasn't the issue; it was the water, tea, coffee, milk and fruit juices that made up the other twelve ounces. As a result, Coke placed vending machines at every street corner, in stores, even in schools. Sales took a quantum leap and far surpassed Pepsi, which has never quite caught up to Coke since. Goizueta recognized that focusing on being better than somebody else is usually not the solution. Most often, it is a situation that is the challenge. Human nature just tends to make it easier for us to consider a person as the problem instead of spending time to analyze the situation.

You may very well have co-workers, friends, and associates who could be a real asset for you, but because you allow yourself to view them as a threat, you miss the benefits they offer. Someone who has already accomplished what you are just getting started on could be a wonderful mentor for you. It just requires your willingness not to feel like it's either them or me. Perhaps you can go further and accomplish more if you could begin to see things in terms of *us*. Sometimes the real measure of our merit comes in learning the lessons that others can teach us. In school, they teach you a lesson, and then you take a test, but in life, you get a test, and then you learn the lesson. You are the greatest indicator of how successfully you will pass your test.

> **NEVER BE AFRAID TO TRY SOMETHING NEW. REMEMBER, AMATEURS BUILT THE ARK; PROFESSIONALS BUILT THE TITANIC.**
>
> - ANONYMOUS -

It is an interesting human dynamic that when faced with something unfamiliar, people typically react in a way that is familiar to whom they are. Regardless of what unfamiliar circumstance they are faced with, most people will do what is common to their habits and personality traits. The woman on the news who cried because of uncertainty over the snow is probably emotional about a lot of things, and that was not an uncanny reaction for her. The people in various neighborhoods who mobilized to work together with what they had are probably very resourceful team players. They accomplish what they are tasked with and achieve their goals. Albeit a bit slower and more unorthodox, they will more likely than not get results.

Designing your life will be enhanced when you can play to your strengths and benefit from the strength of others. Because we tend to rely on our natural impulses, the value of diversity becomes a key factor. When a village of diverse people is faced with unfamiliar circumstances, there are different reactions and viewpoints of what resources they have and what should be done with them. The best practice is typically a compilation of the best ideas and solutions for the situation. So as you look at "what is that in your hand?" don't forget to look at whom you have in your midst and determine the best way to move forward toward your goals.

Lifestyle Lessons

1. You may not have the best of everything you need in order to accomplish a goal, but do your best with what you do have. Don't ever allow your need for perfection to sabotage your pursuit of purpose.
2. Your ability to succeed is limited only by your willingness to improve. Regardless of how difficult your situation is, when your back is against the wall, you are in a perfect position to go forward.
3. Designing your life requires you to identify your existing strengths and improve upon the skills you already possess because knowledge is kept on reserve for those who have a willingness to learn.

Design This

The resolution to any problem is contained within your willingness to resolve it, and the difference between wishing for something and achieving anything is found in your willingness to work for everything.

CHAPTER EIGHT

> **FEAR IS THAT LITTLE DARKROOM WHERE NEGATIVES ARE DEVELOPED.**
>
> - USMAN B ASIF -

I have the honor and privilege of meeting people, literally, from all over the world, and I absolutely love learning about different cultures and hearing of the experiences of others. It provides me with such insight and perspective in a variety of areas. Most people are usually very forthcoming when I meet them and willingly share their concerns, their hopes and dreams, what they love, and where they are in life. Of course, anything they don't willingly tell me, I simply ask. My close friends tease me and say they can always count on me to ask what everybody else wants to know but won't ask. My husband, Bradie, often reminds me once I start asking questions that the person is not under arrest and doesn't need to be interrogated. Because I have such a genuine interest in knowing, the questions come hard and fast sometimes.

I often get so engrossed in whatever the person is telling me that I don't even realize that my questions have treaded into an area that can render some speechless, not because the questions are so personal, but because no one had ever thought to ask before. Without fail, whenever I happen upon a discovery, the same friends who were amazed that I asked come flocking to find out what the answer was. For example, there was a time when I was fortunate enough to interact with a group of ladies from India. I told my American friends that

I had asked them about what we had always described as "dots on their forehead." In one breath, they feigned disbelief that I would actually ask them something like that, and in their next breath my friends were chomping at the bit to know all about it. I explained that it is called a *bindi*, and they come in all different colors in a peel and stick format. The Indian ladies were even gracious enough to offer me an assortment of *bindis* to bring home to America.

With all my international question and answer sessions and years of coaching, I have learned what keeps people from pursuing their goals. Fear. It can cripple goals, destroy dreams and render you immobile from all that you could or should accomplish. I decided to take a really good look at what this fear thing was all about. I knew that *The Designer Life* would require me to understand more about fear, the manifestation of it, and the implications of it. There had to be a way for me to analyze and then categorize the different aspects of a concept that can wreak such havoc. While it won't get your mouth washed out with soap by your grandmother, fear should join the ranks of that other four letter f word that is unacceptable to be uttered.

Human behavior actually only operates in two main emotional realms: one is love and one is fear. Everything else that we experience is based on which emotional realm we are operating from. Love produces things like peace, joy, and kindness. Fear produces things like anger, hatred, and depression. Interestingly enough, when you are operating in the realm of fear, you will find yourself either paralyzed with inactivity or having actions that are ultimately of no real benefit to you or anyone else. Fear actually prohibits growth and the simple truth is, if you are not growing, you are dying. Fear-based intentions will put your life in a holding pattern where you just circle around never really taking off and unable to land.

When I was a little girl, I dreaded having to go to the bathroom in the middle of the night. I was afraid of the dark and didn't want to leave my bedroom and go down the hall alone. I would actually wake my twin brother Frank up and have him escort me to the bathroom. Sounds like a good idea, right? Wrong, because Frank was in another room, so I had to leave my room and walk down the hall anyway. I would literally go to Frank's room and wake him up to walk with me to the bathroom. Then I would insist on him waiting outside the bathroom door until I finished, so he could walk me back to my bedroom. Poor Frank would sometimes be so frustrated. I can remember occasions when he didn't want to oblige me but would simply wake from his sleep and tell me to turn on the light and stop being so ridiculous, but relentlessness is not a new personality trait for me. I would just keep making my request until Frank caved in and accommodated me. During a recent family gathering, we were recounting the experience, trying to figure out what prompted Frank to actually wait for me. Then we laughed hysterically at how outrageous my irrational fear was. How much simpler it would have been to just turn on the light and walk directly to the bathroom.

My behavior was a classic example of senseless behavior that was motivated by fear. Fortunately, I outgrew my fear, and Frank was able to sleep through the night uninterrupted, but when baseless fear follows us into adulthood, the results can be very damaging. Human behaviorist Bill Tancer conducted an extensive online survey to ascertain the top ten fears most Americans have. The list included some predictable fears you would probably be able to guess, such as flying, snakes, and spiders. These fears are typically a result of a negative experience or a traumatic event. The good news is that these types of fears are actually easier to manage because the thing or the activity that causes the fear can be avoided. Also on the list was the fear of public speaking. You might already have known that it is a fear for some people, but it was common enough to be included in the top ten fears. The reason people gave for their fear of public speaking was quite simply being judged. Respondents to the survey indicated that speaking one on one or in a small confined group was fine, but speaking in front of an audience left them vulnerable and open to criticism and judgment.

Another fear in the top ten that you might not have guessed was the fear of success. It sounds almost contradictory, but I have actually encountered it in my coaching. Some people are afraid to succeed. Fear of success is a tricky dynamic because the fear actually stems from the by-product of the success, for example, the goal of losing weight. Most people who want to lose weight would think it was a good thing if they could accomplish their goal, but when you have a fear of success, you are concerned with what happens after the fact. You worry about things like people noticing and making comments, your clothes not fitting, having to pay for a new wardrobe, the expectation of being able to keep the weight off, and possibly becoming a role model for others. The list could go on, but these are just some of the ensuing results you may have to contend with. There is stress and anxiety surrounding the possible outcomes of achieving the goal, which can make you question if it's worth accomplishing. Maybe all you wanted to do was lose weight, but in doing so, you end up with a whole new set of requirements to maintain and manage.

Criticism, judgment, and comments from others are all imposed on us by others. Fear of public speaking and fear of success have something in common. The major deterrents are not internal but external. The real challenge with this component of fear is to become more aware of how much permission you give to others to impose their thoughts and opinions in your life. Even if you are very talented and have ambitious goals, you will be unable to succeed when external fears are outweighing the benefit of accomplishment. *The Designer Life* requires you to take a very close look at what you perceive as the negative by-products compared to the positive results of whatever you are trying to achieve. Unexamined fear has the tendency to grow and multiply, but when fear is faced, it can be conquered.

The latest form of entertainment to sweep American culture is the reality television craze. We watch television shows that display the spectrum of whom we are as a people. *Hoarders* is the show about people who can't throw anything away and over time have run out of living space. As the title suggests, *My Strange Addiction* displays everything from a woman eating toilet paper to the woman who sleeps with her blow dryer running.

Sharing and comparing have become our new national pastime to see if something about me is more odd than something about you. Well, one such show highlighted a gentleman who had a problem with being a picky eater and wanted to overcome his fear of different foods, so every day for a year he forced himself to eat something out of the ordinary like pig ears and bull testicles. I'm not sure where this man was grocery shopping, but the whole purpose was for him to face his fears. Hopefully by facing his fears, he could eliminate them.

There is certainly merit in facing your fear, like turning a light on in the dark so you can see things as they really are. As you are designing your life, it will prove beneficial for you to tackle your fears head-on. An acronym I like to use is that fear is nothing more than false evidence appearing real; furthermore, it almost always projects into some future event. Basically, what frightens us most hasn't even happened yet. Facing your fears will allow you to see clearly what you are perceiving as negative. This will afford you the opportunity to uproot the negatives one by one. Anything that is holding you back can be faced, evaluated, and discarded. Even if you are unable to completely eradicate the negative component of your fear, by facing your fear, you are at least afforded the option to analyze certain elements or areas of concern. Uprooting a negative side effect could mean figuring out how to eliminate it completely, or it could mean just accepting it and learning to live with it.

Fear brought about through the external by-products often imposed by others was a great starting point to begin understanding all of the complexities of this monster concept, but it led me to more questions than answers. I began to consider how some people take on their goals in a fearless way, like a superhero who secretly knows he can dodge bullets, scale walls, and even fly if necessary. Yet others can approach the same goals with fear and trembling, shaking in their boots at the mere thought of accomplishing the goal. Have some of us become conditioned to fear, almost walking in the expectancy of it? I remember when my son, Kyle, was five years old, he wanted to spend time with our family who live in Los Angeles, California. I informed Kyle that I was working on a very important project at work, and it wasn't a good time for me to take a holiday so we could travel to California. He proceeded to ask why he couldn't just go by himself. I really didn't have a plausible answer other than my own secret fear of my only baby flying clear across the country alone.

I decided to check with the airlines what the minimum age requirement was for a child to fly without a parent or guardian. Six was the magic age, and Kyle was just a month shy of his birthday, so I planned the trip for him. I knew I had to manage my fears and not project them onto Kyle, but I had to face my own fear to determine my areas of concern. Instead of just accepting the fear at face value and letting it dictate my decisions, I evaluated my areas of concern. Dismantling the fear and looking at the individual elements created bite size pieces that were easier to digest. I considered that I would be the one to escort Kyle to the plane and put him on a non-stop flight. Once he was on the plane, and 40,000 feet in the air, there wasn't anywhere he could wander off to and possibly get lost. The actual flight wouldn't be a problem for Kyle. At the tender age of six, he was already a veteran air traveler, having made his first cross country flight at a week old. He would probably sleep for the major part of the trip. I further knew he would be met at the gate when he arrived in Los Angeles, and the flight attendants would not release him to anyone other than the designated pick-up person, who would have to present proper identification.

Step by step, I was able to evaluate any area of concern to eradicate the fear completely or decide what I could live with and what would be a deal breaker. My gut reaction may have been fear, but under close examination there was no reason to cave in to the fear and let it dictate my decision. Like most things in life that have the tendency or the potential to hold us back, fear must be managed. When you accept things as they are given to you, you are going to get what you get; however, when you take charge and manage what you will and will not allow, fear, like everything else, has to line up with your vision and goals. We are all responsible for the emotional realm we are operating in and how it will impact our lives. The arrangements were made, and Kyle was excited that he was on his way to what we lovingly refer to as la la land. Two weeks after his sixth birthday, Kyle took his first solo cross country trip. Everything went well. He returned three weeks later exclaiming how much fun he had and how happy he was that he had gone.

As soon as we arrived home, my neighbor came over, and she just happened to ask Kyle, "Were you afraid to get on that big jet and fly so far by yourself?" Kyle just looked at her for a moment and then said, "Afraid of what?" When I reflected on that incident, I realized two very important things. The first lesson I learned was how easily and casually we deposit fear into others that wouldn't otherwise have been there. My neighbor, although well meaning, had phrased her question in such a way that she was feeding Kyle all of her anxiety and fear on a silver tray – serving it up all ready for him to take a heaping portion. If you are not careful, fear can be contagious and spread like wildfire with no hope of being extinguished. The second thing I learned was the importance of not letting fear take hold in the first place.

Kyle hadn't even given thought to the negative, which is where fear is nurtured. He only thought about what he stood to gain from the experience. Was Kyle's approach just a result of childhood innocence? Now, in his late teens, I asked Kyle if he remembered the first time he flew by himself. "Of course, it was a memorable trip," he said. I knew I was safe from projecting any fear onto Kyle at his age and with his experience of travelling, so I pressed further. "Were you in the slightest bit afraid to fly by yourself?" He replied, "No, because getting to Disneyland and Universal Studios was all I could think about." That's it, I thought. This is the methodology for subduing fear: keep your thoughts on the goal – the infamous "keep your eye on the prize" theory. Staying focused on what can be accomplished doesn't leave room for the "what if" of fear.

In order to completely open the kimono and expose fear and all of its tricks, I decided to take a look at some of the situational fears people experience. Fear in the midst of the storm is a real challenge. When life is happening all around you, when the winds and the waves are relentless and tossing you about, it's difficult to think about getting out of the boat and trying to conquer your fear by walking on the water. At times like these, you have to bolster yourself with the antidote of fear, which is faith. Faith is the ability to not rely on logical proof or material evidence. For someone like me, faith is found through spiritual or religious principles; for others, faith is found by focusing on past experiences that might have been difficult but were resolved favorably. Faith might be to believe in something positive, maybe focusing on talents and abilities. Or it may mean simply holding firm to the concept that things always work out in the end, and if they haven't worked out yet, it isn't the end. When you are able to apply faith to your fear in the midst of the storm, you can begin to get out of your boat and walk on water, but remember, even when you walk on water, your feet will still get wet. Things won't be perfect, but it doesn't mean you can't accomplish your goal.

Fear of failure operates in the same dimension as the fear of success. The fear stems from the by-product of a possible outcome and is usually brought about by external factors. Typically, a failure in and of itself is not where the struggle is. The fear is due to the perceived results associated with the unsuccessful attempt at something. When you learn how to focus on what you are trying to accomplish, your failure can become the womb of success. There are countless examples of people who failed many times before they finally accomplished their goals. Colonel Sanders spent two years driving across the United States looking for restaurants to buy his chicken recipe. He was turned down 1009 times before his idea was accepted. This is an example of harnessing the fear and letting it work for you. It wasn't the 1009 failed attempts that were important or what anybody else thought about his efforts. Each time he failed, he became more determined and realized the failed attempt wasn't so bad after all and actually allowed room for growth and improvement. Design your life in such a way that you are able to see a failed attempt as your greatest asset towards your success. That approach will put the fear of failure in its rightful place – out of your life.

The fear of the unknown or the unexpected is a challenge I often hear people wrestling with. When there is the possibility of an unfamiliar outcome, or worse still an uncertain outcome, the result is often fear. There isn't any evidence to suggest any concerns that would trigger the fear. It is simply a matter of not knowing what you don't know. In my experience, the clients who struggle with the fear of the unknown tend to be very structured, almost controlling types of people. I can offer up an amen testimony to people who struggle with the not knowing. I worked hard to overcome my need to organize, control, and know the outcome. My natural tendency has always been to evaluate the outcome in advance with precise detail and little room for error, but I had to learn that life does not come in a nice neat package with a pretty bow tied around it. Sometimes life is sloppy, unpredictable, and an overall hot mess. When I recognized that it was okay to be surprised or caught off guard, that mistakes are made and accidents happen, I began to let go of the need to know and the fear associated with it. I learned that life can be fluid and how to go with the flow. This eliminates, or at least minimizes, the anxiety around the not knowing.

Perhaps your area of struggle is a fear of new experiences. You prefer to keep doing what you have always done. Better the devil you know than the one you don't know. Give some thought to the fact that at some point in your life everything was a new experience. You were born with a blank slate. Over time you began to experience life, but somewhere along the way you became stuck in "that's it." Everything I have done, everything I know is enough. There isn't a need to try something new or do anything different. Plain and simple, the definition of insanity is to continue doing the same thing but expecting a different result. If your life is already perfect, keep on doing what you are doing, and by all means don't try anything new, but if you see any room for improvement in your life, consider the things you do on a daily basis. At one time they were all new experiences, and you survived, perhaps even thrived. That is the approach you want to use when fear creeps in. Tell your fear that you are open to the possibilities of something new and different.

The fear of loss is usually exhibited in people who spend most of their time in the future and are not able to just enjoy their present moments. They speak in terms of "what if" and don't appreciate the "what is." What if I lose my job? What if I lose my home? What if I lose my relationship? This fear is best managed with a change in mindset; simply think in terms of what there is to gain instead of focusing on the potential loss, basically turning everything negative into a positive. Then accept that there are some things, some habits, some situations, and yes even some people, that you should lose.

Whatever area of fear you may contend with, learning more about yourself and recognizing your gifts and talents will work wonders for your ability to manage your fear. I have a little white lap dog named Yogi. Sometimes at night Yogi will see his reflection in the glass door and begin to growl and bark out of fear. He doesn't realize that he is afraid of himself because he doesn't really see himself, but he believes that he sees a perceived threat. Some of us are afraid because we don't really see ourselves. We believe the hype that has conditioned us to think we are not smart enough, talented enough, or whatever area of enough we believe is lacking in our lives. Don't perceive yourself as a threat, but look at your life in terms of potential and possibility. Whatever your goals or opportunities are, remember success is the achievement of something desired and attempted; therefore, you have the opportunity to define success as it relates to your individual circumstance. Whatever you desire to accomplish, do it on your own terms without external opinions and influences. And then don't let fear rest, rule, or abide in your house – where you are paying the cost to be the boss.

CHAPTER NINE

> BECOME WHAT YOU BELIEVE.
>
> - THE BOOK OF MATTHEW -

During the journey of discovering my designer life, I began to look at some of the commonalities of people who were living their best life. Realizing that success is individually defined, I examined the traits and habits of people who had achieved their goals. It is easy to look at people who have fame and fortune, but I think that puts a very limited scope on what success really is. One of my heroes, Booker T. Washington, defined success as the following: "I have learned that success is to be measured not so much by the position that one has reached in life as by the obstacles which he had to overcome while trying to succeed."

SOME PEOPLE DREAM OF SUCCESS WHILE OTHERS WAKE UP AND WORK HARD AT IT.

- ANONYMOUS -

What I love about Mr. Washington's definition of success is that it provides an all- en-compassing approach. Often our culture prescribes the measurements of success, and if we are not careful, we will take it on as the gospel of truth and become like willing disciples, ready to follow it to the ends of the earth. To achieve a certain level of education, or a certain financial status, to drive the right car, live in the right neighborhood, or even have the right look are all means of measuring success based on someone else's definition. But success is really what you become when you have designed your life. Then you are living it out to the best of your ability with dreams that don't expire and goals that are being actualized one step at a time.

By painting success with a broad brush, I looked at people like the young men from the book entitled *The Pact*. It is a true story of three black teenagers from a very poor and rough part of Newark, New Jersey: "A community that had been decimated due to crack cocaine. A place where the sounds of gunshots and screeching cars late at night and before dawn were as familiar to us as the chirping of insects must be to people who live in the country." By their own account, they didn't have anything special going for them except loving mothers (one of whom was a drug user) and above average intelligence. In high school, these young men were skipping class and doing as little schoolwork as possible, but one day a college recruiter came to their high school campus, and the young trio learned of an assistance package for minorities to pursue a career in medicine.

They believed in themselves and their abilities and

thought the opportunity being presented was the way out of their poverty ravaged community, so they developed a pact amongst themselves that basically stated they would help each other at all costs and that none of the three would be allowed to quit until they accomplished the goal. Against some really tough odds, they were able to succeed in accomplishing their goals. Today, all three are practicing doctors and use their resources to help and encourage young people from underprivileged situations.

These young men are not household names and don't have the type of wealth that could support a third world nation, but I consider them a success. They had dreams and goals that were actualized because of several factors, the most important being the belief that they could accomplish what they set out to do. The power of belief is a common denominator of successful people regardless of how it is defined. There is something to be said for people who believe in what they set out to accomplish. They recognize that if they don't believe it, there won't be anybody to believe it for them better than they can believe it for themselves.

DON'T AIM FOR SUCCESS IF YOU WANT IT; JUST DO WHAT YOU LOVE AND BELIEVE IN, AND IT WILL COME NATURALLY.

- DAVID FROST -

Several years ago, during my coach training, I read a book by Edwin H. Friedman entitled *Friedman's Fables*. Although he was an ordained Jewish Rabbi, he focused on enhancing congregational leadership, regardless of the religious faith. One of the areas Rabbi Friedman seeks to strengthen and encourage is the impact of belief at all costs. His story made an impression on me, firstly because I found it to be humorous and secondly because, long after I had chuckled, the implications of the message being conveyed stuck with me and caused me to give real pause to the point of the fable.

One evening a man came home and announced that he was dead. Immediately, some of his neighbors tried to show him what a foolish notion this was. He was walking, and dead men cannot move themselves. He was thinking, his brain was functioning, and he was breathing. That, after all, is the quintessence of living, but none of these arguments had any effect. No matter what reason was brought to bear against his position, no matter how sensible the argument, the man maintained he was dead. He parried their thrusts with ingenious skill. He seemed to have a way of constantly putting the burden of proof on the other. He never quite came right out and said, "Prove it," but that was the message implied, not so much by how he answered as by how he avoided giving any answer at all.

Every now and then someone thought, "Now I've pinned him down," having brought evidence so obvious no one could deny it. But then he would use his trump: "If I am dead, then you don't exist either since surely the living do not traffic with the dead." Eventually most of his friends and neighbors quit arguing and the handful who were left, including his own family, became increasingly afraid. Several reached the same conclusion: He had gone mad or at the very least was suffering from some erratic mental process. Exhaustion from work, perhaps? A brain tumor? He needs a rest. We'll call a doctor, perhaps a psychiatrist, maybe the family physician, or minister.

The man, however, was not upset by these suggestions. He shrugged them off without reply and finally said, "I don't know what's the matter with you all. It is just absurd to think of a dead man as tired, let alone sick."

His wife, almost literally beside herself, took to carrying on a dialogue within. "If he believes this, then how can he say that? If he does that, how can he think this?" As the mixture of fear and frustration thickened, it was finally agreed that outside help must be called in. A psychiatrist was invited over to interview him.

IT'S NOT WHO YOU ARE THAT HOLDS YOU BACK, IT'S WHO YOU THINK YOU'RE NOT.

- ANONYMOUS -

After some preliminary greetings and a few routine questions, the doctor asked to see the man alone. He readily agreed. The two went into another room and closed the door. Now and then an elevated voice could be heard, although nothing could be understood. It was clear, however, that the voice they heard getting louder always belonged to the clinician. Some time later both men emerged. The doctor had his jacket over his arm, his necktie had been loosened and his collar opened (in fact, the button was no longer there). As for the man, he seemed totally unchanged. "Hopelessly psychotic," muttered the psychiatrist. "You will have to have him committed. He has lost all awareness of reality. If you want, I'll call the hospital and see if they have room."

"Now really," said the man calmly, "What kind of therapy would you prescribe for a dead man? Surely, sir, if it were known that you had tried to cure a man who was not even alive, talk about losing one's grip on reality." The doctor started to answer, caught himself, and then, with measured calm, said to the others, "I haven't finished dinner yet. If you want me to call the hospital, give me a ring."

Then a clergyman was sought, but the family minister was unavailable. Who else would be best? The modern kind who had some sophistication about psychological problems, or perhaps a good old fashioned fundamentalist? "Let's fight fire with fire," said someone. As it happened, that evening a well-known evangelist was in town to speak at a nearby theatre. When he heard about the problem he rushed over, thinking how his success might be used to introduce the show. Once again the group was left to strain after the voices behind a closed door. Again, nothing that was audible, again the rising tone, and again never the man's voice rising. This time the clergyman came out alone, stopped, looked at everyone, nervously kissed his little black book, and bolted out the door. Several cautiously peeked into the room; the man was fast asleep.

It was now decided that the family doctor should be called. He had known the man since he was a little boy and, besides being a physician with a reputation for patience and skill, he was respected everywhere for his homey wisdom. He came quickly, and after one or two questions in front of everyone, asked the man in a no-nonsense way, "Tell me, do dead men bleed?" "Of course not," said the man. "Then," said the doctor, "Would you allow me to make a small cut in your arm, say above the elbow? I will treat it; there's no reason to worry about infection. I'll stop the flow immediately, and we can see, once and for all whether you are dead."

"Dead men do not get infections, nor do they bleed, doctor," said the man, as he proceeded to roll up his sleeve. With everyone watching anxiously, the doctor deftly slit the flesh and blood came spurting out. There was a gasp of joy throughout the group. Some laughed, others even applauded, though a few seemed rather to be relieved. The doctor quickly dressed the wound and turned to everyone saying, "Well, I hope that puts an end to this foolishness." Everyone was congratulating the physician when they suddenly realized that the man was headed for the door. As he opened it, he turned to the group and said, "I see that I was wrong." Then, as he turned to leave, he added, "Dead men in fact do bleed."

Now of course this fable is deliberately over exaggerated in an attempt to demonstrate how absurd you can appear when you are willing to have a belief that seems contrary to what the facts or the circumstances dictate. This fable also shows that there are people who can have a belief that is so strong that there isn't anything that can be done to convince them otherwise. Although Rabbi Friedman wrote the fable to depict certain principles, I wanted to really consider that same type of belief that existed in real life. The fable was great for making the point, but I wanted to look at true accounts: real situations and real people with a belief and a desire to accomplish their dreams that was so strong that nothing could deter them.

In 1883, a creative engineer named John Augustus Roebling was inspired by an idea to build a spectacular bridge connecting New York City with Long Island; however, bridge building experts throughout the world thought that this was an impossible feat and told Roebling to forget the idea. It just could not be done. It was not practical. It had never been done before.

Roebling could not ignore the vision he had in his mind of this bridge. He thought about it all the time and believed deep in his heart that it could be done. He just had to share the dream with someone else. After much discussion and persuasion, he managed to convince his son Washington, an up and coming engineer, that the bridge, in fact, could be built.

Working together for the first time, the father and son developed concepts of how it could be accomplished and how the obstacles could be overcome. With great excitement and inspiration, and the headiness of a wild challenge before them, they hired their crew and began to build their dream bridge. The project started well, but when it was only a few months underway a tragic accident on the site took the life of John Roebling. Washington was injured and left with a certain amount of brain damage, which resulted in him not being able to walk or talk or even move.

IT AIN'T WHAT THEY CALL YOU; IT'S WHAT YOU ANSWER TO.

- W C FIELDS -

"We told them so." "Crazy men and their crazy dreams." "It's foolish to chase wild visions." Everyone had a negative comment to make and felt that the project should be scrapped since the Roeblings were the only ones who knew how the bridge could be built. In spite of his handicap, Washington was never discouraged and still had a burning desire to complete the bridge. His mind was still as sharp as ever, and he tried to inspire and pass on his enthusiasm to some of his friends, but they were too daunted by the task. As he lay on his bed in his hospital room, with the sunlight streaming through the windows, a gentle breeze blew the flimsy white curtains apart and he was able to see the sky and the tops of the trees outside for just a moment.

It seemed that there was a message for him not to give up. Suddenly, an idea hit him. All he could do was move one finger, and he decided to make the best use of it. By moving this, he slowly developed a code of communication with his wife. He touched his wife's arm with that finger, indicating to her that he wanted her to call the engineers again. Then he used the same method of tapping her arm to tell the engineers what to do. It seemed foolish, but the project was under way again. For thirteen years, Washington tapped out his instructions with his finger on his wife's arm until the bridge was finally completed.

Today, the spectacular Brooklyn Bridge stands in all its glory as a tribute to the triumph of one man's indomitable spirit and his belief in accomplishing his goals, regardless of the circumstances. At the time, the rest of the world thought Washington was a mad man, yet he would not be deterred from his belief in carrying out his vision. To this very day, millions of vehicles travel across the Brooklyn Bridge because of a man who had belief and perseverance, even under extreme pressure. Often, when we face obstacles in our day-to-day life, our hurdles seem very small in comparison to what many others have to face. The Brooklyn Bridge shows us that dreams that seem impossible can be realized, no matter what the odds are.

SUCCESS IS NOT MEASURED BY WHAT ONE BRINGS, BUT RATHER BY WHAT ONE LEAVES.

- ANONYMOUS -

As I evaluated the power of belief, it naturally ebbed and flowed into yet another commonality of successful people, namely the power of perseverance, even under pressure. With perseverance comes patience. Accomplishing goals takes time, and there really isn't any such thing as an overnight sensation. A person or a business may be discovered overnight, but when you look into the real story behind the story, the process was anything but a one night thing. Even a winner from the *American Idol* television show described the build-up to what seemed like instant fame as her dreams finally came true. The operative word is *finally*. She had been singing since the age of five and practiced her craft every day. The fact that America voted for her one night and she had a recording contract with a major record label the next day didn't mean she had just started her process.

When people are extremely successful we typically only see a snapshot of their process. Unfortunately, this can give a false impression of the perseverance that occurred up until their moment arrived. And when we design our life, we will all have our moment, but not without preparation as well as perseverance under pressure. When you encounter people who are accomplishing their goals and achieving their success, inquire how much of their process was witnessed by the general public. Chances are you will discover the importance of what happens before the success. That's why I believe it is important to focus on the significance of what you are going to accomplish. Perhaps you have decided to pursue advanced education and are working on your degree. Every year you complete school is significant toward your success. For each milestone that is achieved toward that end, there is a reason to feel confident in being one step closer to accomplishing your goal and seeing your dreams made manifest.

AERODYNAMICALLY THE BUMBLEBEE SHOULDN'T BE ABLE TO FLY, BUT THE BUMBLEBEE DOESN'T KNOW THAT SO IT GOES ON FLYING ANYWAY.

- MARY KAY ASH -

Perseverance is what will make the difference in accomplishing your goals rather than just attempting your goals. When you have done everything that needs to be done to design your life, you don't want to give up too soon. Instead, you want to stick with accomplishing your goals and allow your belief to stand against all obstacles and persevere, even under pressure. For when you believe in yourself, your dreams deserve your determination to see them come to fruition at all costs. Famous American humor writer Josh Billings says, "Consider the postage stamp: its usefulness consists in the ability to stick to one thing 'til it gets there!" When you are living out your *Designer Life* goals, I would encourage you to take purpose like a postage stamp and stick to your goals until you get there.

OUR GREATEST WEAKNESS LIES IN GIVING UP. THE MOST CERTAIN WAY TO SUCCEED IS ALWAYS TO TRY JUST ONE MORE TIME.

- THOMAS A EDISON -

Sometimes our best examples of how to go about doing something come from learning what not to do. And when you can learn what not to do based on someone else who already made the mistake, count it to your credit that there is one less mistake you have to pay for. During the 1800's, when gold was discovered in the Coloma Valley, California experienced what became known in American history as the Gold Rush. This was a significant discovery as it played a major role in the development of California. Tens of thousands of people came from all over the world to dig for the gold that had been discovered. Many American millionaires were created. San Francisco grew from a small settlement to the booming metropolis it is known for today, and California was able to join the union of the states in 1850.

During this time, there were two brothers who sold all their belongings in order to head to California and prospect for gold. They discovered a vein of the shining ore, staked a claim, and proceeded to get the gold ore out of the mine. At first all went well, but then the vein went dry, and the brothers were unable to get the gold. They believed they had come to the end of the road, so after a few unsuccessful attempts, the brothers gave up in disgust. They sold their equipment and claim to the land for a few hundred dollars and took the train back home in defeat. The man who bought the claim hired an engineer to examine the rock strata of the mine. The engineer advised him to continue digging in the same spot where the former owners had left off. Three feet deeper, the new owner struck gold and became one of the American millionaires that resulted from the Gold Rush.

YOUR PERSEVERANCE IS THE MEASURE OF FAITH IN YOURSELF.

- ANONYMOUS -

Surely, we can all see that perseverance would have paid off for the brothers, and reading about their account, with the benefit of history, makes it easy to recognize they should have continued to pursue their goals. But when history has to write your story, will it demonstrate what not to do, or will you become an example of what it means to believe and persevere, regardless of what it looks like? You are designing your life; therefore, you get to decide how to shape your own story of sticking with your goals despite the odds and the obstacles.

Perhaps your story will look like the American inventor Thomas Edison who, despite a hearing problem, changed the world with some of his inventions or the American actor and orator James Earle Jones who had a terrible problem with stuttering but had the belief and perseverance to overcome his challenge and accomplish his goals. Maybe your story will be similar to the British-born gold-medal-winning Olympian athlete Derek Redmond who tore his hamstring in the middle of a race but persevered through the pain and the pressure to complete his lap. After the Olympics, a doctor told Derek that he would be unable to compete professionally again, but Derek had been plagued with injuries before and was determined to follow his love of sport. When he did begin competing professionally again, he sent a photo to the doctor who had told him he would not be able to perform at a professional level again. When I think about Derek's story, it reminds me of former British Prime Minister Margaret Thatcher who always said, "You may have to fight the same battle more than once to win it."

I love sharing with my American audiences how much I learn when I travel to other countries. During my first visit to West Africa, I noticed that although the area was rich with diamond mines, the professional women I was meeting did not wear much diamond jewelry. Of course, I had to gain a better understanding regarding this obvious absence of any *bling bling* since we all know how the ladies in the West feel about our diamonds. Fortunately, it didn't take long to gain some perspective and understanding related to my question, which was based solely on curiosity.

One day while I was on duty in my observation laboratory, which also serves as the hotel lobby, I watched a very sharp and well-dressed business woman come into the hotel lobby equipped with the best in designer clothes, shoes, and bag. I smiled politely, as is my habit, so I can begin to engage a perfect stranger in a dialogue of discovery. Her name was Nicole, and she had actually arrived thirty minutes early for a business meeting. Jackpot! A friendly person with time to kill. After I had engaged in small talk with Nicole and answered her questions about America, I shared with her my observation regarding the diamond jewelry. Her initial reaction was laughter, but then she told me quite directly, "You Westerners are obsessed with diamonds, but you must remember they really are nothing more than rocks that have been pressured and polished." I love it when people give it to me straight without hesitation, and I thanked Nicole for her profound honesty.

> **THE GEM CAN NOT BE POLISHED WITHOUT FRICTION, NOR MAN PERFECTED WITHOUT TRIALS.**
>
> - CHINESE PROVERB -

After my encounter with Nicole I began to really think about what she said and how true her statement was. Most of us have been socialized into the beauty of diamonds and don't consider that they are mere rocks that have undergone pressure and polishing to become what we consider precious and valuable. As I contemplated this concept, I thought about how our lives can reflect the same principle. Sometimes it is through some pressure and some polishing that the ordinary can become the extraordinary, so remember, when you are in your process and you persevere under pressure, that without it, you would just be a rock, but when you stick with it, you will be an invaluable gem.

The concept of believing you can achieve and being willing to stick with your goals is a fundamental part of designing your life. It is a principle that I am firmly committed to, and I encourage audiences and clients to embrace it with all their heart. Often times we read accounts of famous people and still find it hard to accept that they are just like us. Surely Thomas Edison, James Earle Jones, Prime Minister Thatcher, the people who built bridges, and Olympic athletes have been successful in their own right, but they are different. There must have been something else that we don't know that was the determining factor in the achievement of their goals.

Because I feel so strongly about reaching people with the message of belief and perseverance, I want to share with you this story that I know as fact. It is not an account in a history book, but I have witnessed it myself. I share it with you, not because I want you to believe that I am a candidate for mother of the year or that I gave birth to a wonder child, but to encourage each person who wonders if he can really believe something at all costs and stick with it until his goals are accomplished; I want to share this with each person who wonders if the ordinary can become the extraordinary when he dares to believe in himself and his abilities. If that person is you, please know that *yes you can*.

My son, Kyle, developed a love for the game of basketball and proclaimed he was going to play Division

1 basketball in the top conference in the country. This sounded well and good as long as Kyle kept in mind that he and several million other young guys had the same dream of playing at the highest level of amateur sports in the country. Throughout high school, Kyle kept his eye on the prize. When other teenagers were at the mall having fun with friends, Kyle was in the gym practicing. In the evenings, when the family would gather and watch television, Kyle was doing pushups and all types of calisthenics to improve his strength.

Countless times, I had to remind Kyle not to dribble tennis balls in the house, which is what he practiced with because a tennis ball is more challenging to control when dribbling. As Kyle would remind me, "When you can master control of two tennis balls simultaneously, handling one basketball becomes easy." When Kyle began his senior year of high school, it was time for a decision regarding college. I knew how much Kyle wanted to accomplish his goal, but I must admit I wanted Kyle to play it safe and just focus on his academics. The odds were against Kyle's basketball dream, just simply based on the millions of young men competing for less than two hundred spots.

As the year advanced, Kyle's friends were all accepting college offers and making their decisions about where they would attend school. One month before Kyle graduated high school, he still had not decided where he was going to attend college. He had gone on a college visit where they offered him admission and a basketball scholarship, and he turned it down. At this point, everything I had taught Kyle about belief in his abilities and perseverance was going out the window. I was beginning to do everything I had always said not to do. Since I believe in transparency, I will admit that I was so stressed I needed someone to coach me through the day. I couldn't believe we were down to the wire with no college choice, and this child of mine was turning down scholarship offers.

I confronted Kyle and told him his dream was getting a bit ridiculous at this point. I said that being able to play college basketball was good enough, and he needed to count it all joy, accept it as success, and get on with it. His response was, "That may be success as you see it, but it is not how I see it. I have believed for more than five years that I can accomplish my goal. I am not going to give up. Because if I don't believe that it will happen, then it won't."

Two weeks before Kyle graduated from high school, and his mother was on the verge of a major melt down, he received a call from the coach of his travel basketball team. The coach told Kyle that he had arranged for him to go down to Georgia Tech and meet with the coaches and try out for the team. Years of belief, preparation and perseverance were finally going to boil down to a few hours of pressure in a gymnasium. Well, all went well, and they welcomed Kyle to the university and the basketball team with open arms! So Kyle's belief, and perseverance under pressure, paid off as Georgia Tech is Division 1 basketball in the top conference in the country.

YOU HAVE TO EXPECT THINGS OF YOURSELF BEFORE YOU CAN DO THEM.

- MICHAEL JORDAN -

Kyle believed at all costs, even when sadly enough he was getting pressure from his own mother to redefine success. He was not willing to alter his plan or give up on his dream. Even though I had taught Kyle the principles he stood by, it is important that he had to believe it for himself — because there came a time when even I was not willing to continue on with the belief in his goal. What I want you to take away from this story is that Kyle does not have something that the history books don't tell you about. I gave birth to him, and I know his imperfections and flaws as well as anyone. Kyle is just like the person who is reading this and wants to accomplish a goal. He is a young man who believed he could achieve, and against the odds he was willing to persevere under pressure to accomplish his goal.

Lifestyle Lessons

1. The power of belief is a common denominator found within successful people. You are the person that is best equipped to believe in your ability to succeed in spite of the obstacles.
2. Success has a price you must be willing to pay and a process you must be willing to complete because perseverance is the real game changer between attempting and accomplishing.
3. Designing your dreams deserves your determination because it is your destiny that is being shaped. People pleasers seek permission, but God pleasers take authority.

Design This

Designing your life isn't easy, but it is fulfilling. You will encounter criticism and doubt along your journey, but faith in your goals will stand above the pettiness, against the odds, and under pressure.

CHAPTER TEN

When I began to design my life, patience is an area where I really struggled. My personality and natural tendencies did not bode well for waiting. I wanted answers like yesterday and results by the start of the business day tomorrow. Well, life doesn't work that way, and I had to learn how to balance aggressively seeking to accomplish my goals with relaxing and enjoying the process. For me, this proved to be a great challenge. In general, I think Americans tend to be more impatient than most. Our culture thrives on deadlines and stress. For us, faster is always better, and the more we can cram onto our already overcrowded calendars the better. Busy has become the new standard of success. Polite small talk at a business meeting or any other event where professionals are gathered will sound like a commercial for the United States Army whose motto is, "We do more before 9 AM than most people do all day."

The busier you are the better, and bragging about everything you still need to get done has become more prestigious than name dropping or casually mentioning your Ivy League education. It is no wonder I struggled with taking a deep breath and spending time learning how to design my life. With *busy* and *success* becoming synonymous, how do you practice patience in the midst of it all? In the land of instant where everything from the internet to the microwave is constantly being improved upon to make it even faster than before, who has time for patience? If America, in general, thrived on being busy and getting it done yesterday, you could call me "stressed on steroids." Microwaves may be getting faster, but in order to properly design my life, I needed a slow cooker approach that would slowly but surely accomplish the task.

PATIENCE IS THE COMPANION OF WISDOM.

- ST AUGUSTINE -

I mentioned in previous chapters how much there is to learn from tuning into life and letting the lessons come from ordinary life experiences. As I always remind myself that in school you get a lesson, and then you take a test, but in life you get a test, and then learn the lesson, so it happened several years ago. During spring break, my husband, Bradie, and I decided we would do something as a family since we had both been so busy, and we also wanted some time together with our son. I had my sights set on a beach vacation where I could read and relax and where the most challenging thing I had to do for the day was to decide what I wanted for dinner. However, Kyle had a different plan, and he was able to convince his dad, so democratically, my idea would not win. As a side note, democracy only goes so far, but I am completely comfortable with a dictatorship in matters pertaining to Kyle!

Instead of a nice resort with fun and sun, something that was comfortable and familiar to me, my family wanted to go indoor skydiving. Now I must admit that I found myself wondering, "Who is this person I have molded and shaped since birth who has such a penchant for what can best be described as *thrill seeking*?" I don't know what surprised me more, my son for thinking of the idea or my husband for agreeing. Not wanting to appear uncooperative, or worse still, seem afraid to try something new, I agreed to the dive. Before the indoor dive, we went to a class that taught us all the techniques, postures, and hand signals required for the dive. That was when I learned that each jump into the wind tunnel would feel like a free fall from an airplane.

Initially, I had questioned my family for suggesting such an activity, but when I heard that the jump was the same as a free fall from an airplane, I questioned myself. What was I thinking to agree to such madness? As if the idea of the jump wasn't crazy enough, I had actually paid money to take on something that seemed outrageous at best and insane at its worst. The most daring thing I had ever done related to a flight was taking my chances with whatever food was being served because I had not ordered a special meal in advance. There had never been a time in my life when I had even remotely speculated what it would feel like to free fall from a plane at any height – let alone that high in the air.

Bradie dived first, and he did well with everything we had learned in the training sessions. Kyle dived next and, wouldn't you know it, he glided through the air like a seasoned veteran. Apparently, he had really paid attention to the class instructors. He looked just like the demonstration video they showed on how to have a successful dive. I was the last person in our family to dive, and let's just say if Kyle looked like what to do, I looked like what not to do. I was in the wind tunnel fighting and chopping through the air, trying to grab on to something that obviously wasn't there. At one point, I turned upside down, trying to get out of the wind chamber. My antics drew the attention of several employees who seemed to find comic relief in my performance. The training instructor kept flashing me the signals for relax, have faith, stop fighting it. Those signals seemed like a good idea sitting in a classroom with a desk, a chair, and the ground firmly under my feet. Free falling in the air, with my stomach in my throat, I had a hand signal of my own I wanted to share back with that instructor, but crass is not my style.

> **IF YOU DO THINGS WELL, DO THEM BETTER. BE DARING, BE FIRST, BE DIFFERENT, BE JUST.**
>
> - ANITA RODDICK -

When our dives were all completed, Bradie and Kyle couldn't say enough about how much they had enjoyed the experience. I just thanked God it was over. Then I made a mental note not to consult with the two daredevils for the next family holiday. As we prepared to leave, one of the employees from the facility informed us that they had video taped our dive and had it available for us to take home on DVD. "Well, wasn't that nice of you," I politely replied, as if I ever really wanted to relive the experience. Kyle put the nail in the proverbial coffin when he indicated that it was great they had recorded me as he wanted to send the DVD to the *America's Funniest Home Videos* television show. To this day, my family still wonders what ever happened to that DVD!

About two weeks after my indoor dive experience, I

was speaking to a Toastmaster's group. The session was for corporate employees who were not accustomed to speaking in public but needed to gain some proficiency in the matter. A very soft-spoken young lady tentatively raised her hand to ask a question. She indicated that she was an engineer and was much more comfortable with computers than having to present to a group. She asked me what she should do to overcome her fear. Without hesitation, I told her to make sure she was confident in her subject matter, to take a deep breath, to relax, and then to have faith in her ability to present the information.

And then it hit me. It was what the dive instructors were trying to get me to do. They hand signaled for me to relax, have faith, and stop fighting it, for when I was in an unfamiliar situation and not sure of my surroundings, I panicked. Yet, when asked by someone how I would handle something that is very comfortable and familiar to me, I gave the exact same advice. Life lesson number ninety-nine was in full effect that day. This was going to really help me with *The Designer Life*. Learning how to navigate through unchartered waters would be invaluable for the process, but I wanted to learn how to do more than just survive the unfamiliar and the uncomfortable. I wanted to be able to relax, have faith, and not fight the situation, but go with it.

In doing so, there was the potential to learn and grow, and perhaps even to enjoy the ride.

When I began to consider the potential this approach could offer, I became excited about all the possibilities. Bradie, Kyle, and I were all in the same circumstance in the wind tunnel. It was new and unfamiliar to all of us, yet they came through their experience excited and feeling glad about the opportunity for something thrilling and different while I came through wishing I had never done it. Life can become a matter of how we go through the tunnel because that will determine our outcome. The ability to remove the barriers and release the self-imposed limitations on my life was going to be the coup de grace of designing my life, and I wanted to take this thought process and run with it. I began to think of an encounter I had more than twenty-five years ago that really spoke to my new discovery. It's amazing how long it can sometimes take for us to connect the dots in life, but I remain ever grateful that when I get it, I really get it. Then, if it is valuable to me, I want to help everybody else get it.

When I was a university student, home on a summer break, I was in downtown Philadelphia having lunch with Dad. When we got ready to leave the restaurant, two men noticed Dad and came over to greet us. Apparently, they had been homicide detective trainees when Dad was retiring. They spoke to me and complimented Dad by telling me how much they appreciated him. They said that all Dad's advice and willingness to help them out as they began their careers had made a real difference for them. They even joked about Dad being the one to make sure they had coffee and doughnuts for the morning autopsies.

The moment we were out of the restaurant, I couldn't wait to ask Dad about what I had just heard. I knew that Dad was an interesting character, but this was a real eye opener. "Dad, you had coffee and doughnuts at an autopsy? Why on earth would you do something like that?" I have already described my father to you, the reader, so hold that thought as I give you his response. Dad simply looked at me like he didn't know why I was so surprised, shrugged his shoulders and said, "Why not?" Yes, it really was just that simple for him.

When I probed further, he indicated that the homicide autopsies were normally performed very early in the morning. Because crime doesn't sleep, sometimes the detectives had not either. The coffee and doughnuts were a nice pick-me-up or probably more accurately a sugar rush. Then Dad went on to have one of his Rodin moments as the family lovingly jokes about his philosophical tendencies. He explained that spending time wondering why you should or should not do something will more often than not convince you not to do something. So rather approach things from the "why not?" perspective; it makes it much easier to move forward with what you want to do and leaves you less vulnerable to playing it safe and following the crowd. I am sure that the lesson Dad conveyed some twenty-five years ago had some impact because, for the most part of my life, I have not felt led to follow the crowd and have considered myself an independent thinker.

EXPERIENCE IS A COMB WHICH NATURE GIVES US WHEN WE ARE BALD.

- ENGLISH PROVERB -

For some reason, as I was putting together the components of designing my life, the lesson Dad was conveying decades ago made a lot more sense. And more importantly, I could see the practical application of it. Flipping the script and looking at life through the lens of "why not?" would allow me to see things completely differently. Sure enough, when I began to put this into practice, I felt like a whole new world opened up to me. Consider in your own life how you can deploy a "why not?" attitude. In new situations, instead of panicking and asking, "Why am I here? Why am I doing this? Why me?" just ask yourself, "Why not?" Approaching a career change, launching out into a new business venture, advancing your education – why not?

People pleasers can spend an entire lifetime seeking the approval of others and become paralyzed with examining the why of anything they consider doing. But when you take the liberty to design your own life, you owe it to yourself to move forward and choose from all the possibilities that exist. Instead of seeking permission, just be prepared to ask for forgiveness if somehow you offend someone or overstep your bounds. I have learned that in the grand scheme of things, life is a relatively short journey. There is so much to do and see when you open yourself up to all the wonderful opportunities that can be yours if you are willing to walk into life, so there is no time to waste seeking permission from others to enjoy yourself, to take on new experiences, to attempt the probable, and to accomplish the impossible.

While I was putting the finishing touches on my process of designing my life, I had an experience that allowed me to see the bigger picture of what I was doing. There is nothing like a first-hand account of something to really bring home the message. I was having what I thought was a stressful day. My husband Bradie was returning home from a trip, but his connecting flight was delayed. We were scheduled to have dinner in our home later in the evening for some of his business associates, and he would barely have enough time to get home before our guests arrived. The caterer for the dinner had inadvertently scheduled his workers to arrive at my home on the incorrect date but felt confident he could rebound and resolve the situation. As this mini-drama was unfolding, Kyle yelled to me from the terrace level of our home that there was water on the floor. Of course my first reaction was, "Just wipe it up." But he yelled more frantically, and as I decided to go downstairs to see what the matter was, there was water on the floor alright, up to my ankles to be more specific. As I walked around to inspect, the carpet was squishing under my feet. I walked to the utility area of the house realizing that one of the air conditioning units or water heaters must be the culprit. Deductive reasoning is a good thing as you never know when it may come in handy. My suspicions were confirmed; the water heater had a leak.

I walked back upstairs and began to take a mental inventory of the damage. Wasn't this just what I needed on a day like today? Then my phone rang and I thought, "Now what? Isn't everything I've been handed, all before 12 noon, quite enough for one day?" It was a call from Regina, my friend Vanessa's sister. Just based on her hello, she didn't sound good. I heard stress, tension, and fear in her voice. Coupled with the fact that Regina doesn't normally call me, I became a bit concerned. "What's up?" I asked her. "It's Vanessa. She has had a cardiac arrest, she's in a coma, and the doctors indicated that she is clinically dead. She is currently on life support, but the emergency room physician has advised the family to prepare for the possibility of death or severe and permanent brain damage."

So much for what I thought was important up until that moment. My mind started racing. How could this happen? Vanessa is only a few years older than I am, and we are still young. I had just talked to her the night before, and she sounded perfectly fine. How could this happen to someone like Vanessa, the dearest friend anyone could ever hope to have? As mentioned in Chapter One, Vanessa and I have been through a lot together. Actually that was an understatement. Vanessa could set the standard of what a true friend is. When I moved to Georgia, I had not designed my life yet and still had quite a few quirks and habits. Controlling and anal were leading the pack of things I had not yet learned how to manage. So Vanessa, who knows me better than most, devised a plan to ease my transition. I did not want the house movers to unpack anything in my new house because I am so particular and didn't want my things placed in a way that was not to my satisfaction. In order to prepare for the work that was ahead of me, I thought a relaxing holiday would renew my strength to take on the task of unpacking.

When the moving trucks left our home in Texas, I boarded a plane with Bradie to spend two weeks in the Caribbean. Vanessa devised a plan without my knowledge and coordinated with Bradie to meet the moving company at our new house in Georgia. She single-handedly unpacked the entire contents of our home. When I came back from vacation and arrived at my new home, all prepared to take on the task of unpacking, Vanessa greeted me at the door. I was happy to see her but wondered why she wasn't at home in Texas. And as I walked into my house I began to understand what was really going on. Everything was completely in place. The china was in the cabinet, the lamps were in place, sheets were on the bed, even towels were hanging from the rack. "Surprise!" Vanessa shouted. I didn't have to stress about getting anything unpacked. She was so excited and happy to do it. It was her way of being there for me because she felt that I had always been there for her. This is the type of friendship Vanessa and I share.

I was having trouble keeping pace with my own thoughts.

Regina knew that Vanessa would want me to know right away, so she had called but didn't have any more details. She would keep me informed. I thought about the time I was panicking about my abnormal white blood cell reading and how Vanessa just calmly told me she was going to pray for me. Turn about is fair play, and I began to pray without ceasing for Vanessa. My friend needed a miracle, and I was going to stand firm on the fact that she was as good a candidate as anyone to receive it. Several days later, Vanessa became a medical miracle. She would make a full recovery with no brain damage.

During her recovery period, I stayed in Texas with Vanessa for about three weeks. We had a wonderful time relaxing and just enjoying each other's company. Vanessa had to make lifestyle adjustments, and I was just the person to help her find humor in the process. Jokingly, I had to ask Vanessa the burning question that most people won't ask but everyone wants to know. I asked if she had seen a bright white light, or if she had floated outside of her body, maybe even been transported somewhere, like in the movies when people are near death, but then they live and recount all of these experiences that happened while the doctors were working to save their lives. Vanessa merely chuckled and told me that Hollywood does a great job over-dramatizing just about everything.

But then I asked her a serious question that I thought would be the most insightful. "Now what? What becomes different about your life once you have literally died, and then you are given a second chance to live?" Vanessa said that she just wanted to live in the present moment, to truly enjoy each day one day at a time and not wish it away with tomorrow. This was good, really good. I began to think about this as it related to designing my life. Goals are good, dreams are great, but in the process of accomplishment there has to be enjoyment. Each day is a gift, a present to be enjoyed.

> **GIVE YOUR ENTIRE ATTENTION TO WHAT GOD IS DOING RIGHT NOW, AND DON'T GET WORKED UP ABOUT WHAT MAY OR MAY NOT HAPPEN TOMORROW.**
> - THE BOOK OF MATTHEW -

I began to think of my own life and that of my many coaching clients. How much time do we spend looking toward the future and what needs to be done, and then worrying about what would happen if it didn't get done? Then we try to sort out what to do about what didn't get done. For all the time that is spent organizing the future, an equal amount of time should be spent just enjoying the moment. The saying that Rome wasn't built in a day holds true for *The Designer Life*. Everything great you want to accomplish does not happen all at once, and it's okay. Enjoy what is being built as it happens. You don't have to wait and take it all in some day. Turn your someday into today. This is the day – enjoy the moment.

During a recent flight to Johannesburg I got up to stretch and walk around the plane. Seventeen hours of flying is quite a bit of time to spend on one aircraft, even for the most seasoned air traveler. As I was walking in the aisle, I encountered a lady from Europe travelling with her two young children. They were native Spanish speakers and the youngsters were eager to practice their English. Although my Spanish was a bit rusty, I obliged in polite small talk. The young girl eagerly asked, "Are we almost here yet?" Recognizing the complexities of English I thought about how to explain the difference between *here* and *there*. In Spanish here and there are very basic and don't take on different parts of speech with tense changes to consider. I laughed at the enthusiasm of the young girl because she didn't care to learn the difference; she just wanted an answer to her question.

As I returned to my seat, I thought about the concept of being here yet. Of course it is grammatically incorrect, but the implications are interesting. Living a life on purpose, by design, should always have you in the here because wherever you are in the present moment is your here. Think of the maps found in a mall with the icon that says, "You are here." And while your *yet* has not happened, it is still important to recognize and take in your *here*, not just wishing life away until you get to *there*. When you think in terms of here and there, the there speaks to an arrival. But *The Designer Life* isn't a destination; it's a way of living life.

Life can be designed based on thoughts, attitudes and decisions. But what is the real benefit in designing something that you don't enjoy? Setting a goal and accomplishing it, dreaming a dream and watching it come to pass are amazing experiences. They just need to be balanced with enjoying the journey; therefore, *The Designer Life* could never be destination focused. It is a lifestyle, one that needs a very active component of stopping to smell the roses and enjoying things big and small. Watching a beautiful sunrise or sunset should have pleasure and meaning in and of itself. Sharing a warm cup of tea with a loved one on a cool winter's day is to be appreciated in that very moment.

The Designer Life is yours to embrace with child-like wonder and enthusiasm for all things possible. A bright future doesn't need permission from a dim past. Your life is a journey that can only best be travelled by you. Stay focused on where you want to go in life, and don't let anyone else determine your pace. Take time to enjoy each day as your gift, and tune into the simple pleasures of life. These are all the components of getting off the sidelines of life and getting into the game. So do your best, leave it all on the court, play hard, and make the decision to win.

Lifestyle Lessons

1. Goals are good, dreams are great, but it is the process that will make you better and provide you with the best possible outcome.
2. Your point of view may change, but your vision must remain constant, and your ambition must be tempered by wisdom and guided by patience.
3. Being busy is not synonymous with being on purpose because focusing on the future must be balanced with enjoying the moment.

Design This

Putting things in perspective will make your process more meaningful and your journey more enjoyable. Learn from the lessons of your past, enjoy the experiences of your present, and plan for a brighter future.

CPSIA information can be obtained
at www.ICGtesting.com
Printed in the USA
BVHW07s0029180918
527751BV00011B/86/P